D1282914

Open School

*The experience of 1964–1970
at Wyndham School, Egremont,
Cumberland*

For Nicola
(1944-1969)

Open School

The experience of 1964–1970
at Wyndham School, Egremont,
Cumberland

John Sharp M.A.

J. M. DENT & SONS LTD
LONDON

Made in Great Britain
at the
Aldine Press, Letchworth, Herts
for
J. M. DENT & SONS LTD
Aldine House, Bedford Street, London

First published in this edition 1973

Boards: ISBN: 0 460 09545 5
Limp: ISBN: 0 460 09564 1

Contents

Acknowledgments

Grateful acknowledgment is made to the Cambridge University Press for their permission to quote from *Life in the Middle Ages* by G. C. Coulton, to the Oxford University Press for their permission to quote from the abridged edition of *The Study of History* by Arnold Toynbee, and to W. R. Elliot for permission to use an extract from his speech to the Headmasters' Association in April 1969.

Foreword

If Dunning were a member of a staff room today rather than of the House of Commons in 1780 his celebrated motion to the Crown might run: 'The influence of the Head has increased, is increasing and ought to be diminished.'

At the present time in our educational history sensible authorities are leaving more and more to governors of schools who in their wisdom are leaving more to the heads whom they exist to help.

What are the Heads doing? They, if they are wise, are leaving more to their staffs who in their turn are passing responsibility to pupils, much of whose education should consist of learning to bear it.

Mr Sharp's chapter on streaming provides an illuminating example of how a head and his staff arrive at decisions. First there is the educational thinking and then there follows careful experiment grounded in experience and undertaken in the light of high principle.

But perhaps even more significant is the absence of the first person singular. There is no 'What I did'; it is all 'What we decided to do'. Within this mature professional discussion the Head established the conditions under which his own ideas and those of his colleagues can be discussed and translated into acceptable action. The influence of the Head has increased and is increasing. In sharing it Mr Sharp shows how it can and ought to remain distinguished.

Good schools are good because of the people who create and run them. The school about which this book is written is still struggling to find the best way of putting into practice the principle enunciated by Thring of Uppingham: 'All can walk part of the way with genius.'

In the next twenty years the country will see a development in our secondary schools similar to that which the last twenty have seen in the primary schools. Those who are called to play a part in this development should profit from reading this wise and timely book.

A B CLEGG
(Sir Alec Clegg)
Education Officer, West Riding of Yorkshire.

Preface

It is a truism that the last decade has seen a ferment of new
ideas in education. In 1959, in *Educating One Nation*,[1] I was
urging the case for comprehensive schools. No wonder that the
book is out of print now! The fact of reorganisation may be
the largest single change in the secondary field but the curricular
advances sponsored by the Schools Council, the Nuffield
Foundation and others, the evolution of the Certificate of
Secondary Education with its new approach to examining, the
movement towards unstreaming, the vast expansion and
changes in Sixth Forms which necessarily bring other developments (casting doubt, for example, on such long-established
features of school life as prefectship)—all these and many other
changes are essentially new since 1960. But some of them are
by no means universally accepted. Education is a conservative
industry. This book is intended as a contribution towards new
thinking although few, if any, of its ideas are not already
practised in some schools.

It has also another, and perhaps more honourable, purpose.
This is to express thanks to those who established Wyndham
School, Egremont, in 1964—by indicating some of the things
which their far-sighted plans and generous support have made
possible even in the short life of the school. Gordon Bessey,
Director of Education for Cumberland, and his Committee,
with Douglas Dickenson, County Architect, must head the list.
A very high place is taken by Michael Harrison, now Director
for Sheffield but formerly Assistant Director in Cumberland.
They planned forward-looking premises (if here and there so
unusual as to be maddening to the users!). Their plans, the
freedom which they encouraged, and the circumstances which
provided a genuine comprehensive intake, not creamed by any
day school, gave us a rare opportunity. They made it possible
to recruit a remarkable staff. Margaret Lorenz and Dick

Copland were the first. They worked with me as Deputy Heads to bring up our common brain-child. Now they lead comprehensive schools in Devon and Durham. To them, to many colleagues and to many others, including Governors and parents, a debt of gratitude is owed. I have tried to pay a little of it here.

The book deals generally with problems of secondary education and often tells how we approached them at Wyndham. In different circumstances other solutions might be more appropriate. I certainly do not wish to suggest that in any educational problem there can be only one way. But I hope that our experience may be of interest to others who have the welfare of children at heart. It may help to suggest that a new age demands new thinking in schools as everywhere else.

There are two other points which, although purely personal, I think I should make. The first is that, as one of H.M. Inspectors of Schools in the period 1947–58, I had an opportunity denied to most headmasters of surveying the whole field of English education. (One year was spent abroad as a Travelling Fellow of the Nuffield Foundation.) The second is that, shortly after completing the manuscript of this book, I left Wyndham School. This was a traumatic decision arrived at very slowly. After seven years in Egremont I had seen some of the original eleven-year-olds enter the Upper Sixth and most of my hopes for the school fulfilled. Because of my age, this was the last possible moment at which I could hope for a new appointment so that I could not do as I should have preferred—to stay for another two or three years only. My fear was that the young school should ever cease to go forward; still worse, that it could look to me for a lead which I might be no longer capable of giving. With inner sadness but compensating relief, I handed over the direction to Peter Brown, lately headmaster of Walworth School. He has given approval for the publication of the book. I myself am happy with a very different but attractive challenge in the headship of Bicester School, Oxfordshire.

Bicester, January 1971   John Sharp

NOTE

1 Sharp, John, *Educating One Nation* (Max Parrish, 1959).

Chapter One

Towards a new kind of secondary school

Two centuries ago the historian Gibbon was much offended by the practice of some undergraduates at Oxford who, he said, were boorishly wearing their hair short. We start from this remark simply as a reminder that things really do change, even if sometimes only back to an earlier fashion.[1]

In 1867 the Parliament of the richest nation on earth considered, but rejected, introducing some compulsory schooling for all, under a Bill 'For the education of the poor'. At the time this title seems to have covered some nine-tenths of all our children. That was the background to the Forster Act of 1870. It was not until 1902 that we proposed to set up secondary schools to be run at public expense for anybody—and, in practice, for only a very few. How enormously the world has changed since then—or even since 1920, when only six in every hundred of English children were in school beyond the age of fourteen. Slightly more than this proportion now goes to university. In recent years great changes have come over secondary education. But close examination may suggest that they have been too small, often brought about only by the pressure of events, and frequently looked upon by their agents as defeats rather than as wise decisions. So firmly fixed has been the idea of a secondary school evolved by an earlier generation.

If we should speak, in Platonic phrase, of 'the idea of a secondary school', what springs to mind? Or, to be fair, what would have sprung not long ago to the mind of most of us? Perhaps something like this: a relatively small institution, almost certainly for one sex alone, preferably residential and in the country, looking rather to the past and to its great traditions than to the future with its varied challenge. It would be

1

segregated from the world in a spiritual sense and, in the material, removed from contact with the crowd by walls (probably), trees (possibly) and playing fields (almost certainly). The latter would bulk large in the life of the pupils, even if these were girls. If they were boys, they would also be expected to be keen on boxing and to join the Cadet Force. All would wear a uniform, perhaps in order to make detection easier if they should offend or abscond, but certainly to distinguish them from scholars elsewhere. This followed not only the regimental ideal but also that which says: 'No education is good enough for my child unless it can be shown that someone else's child receives a less good one.' The uniform might well consist of an Edwardian sports blazer and a nineteenth-century cricket cap (recalling that a century ago all but the very poorest people covered their heads for all outdoor activities and for some indoor ones as well, notably smoking and going to bed). Finally, the school's régime would be firmly based on competition. This reflected both the idea that education is not interesting (so that children must be prodded into it by some external stimulus) and the ethos of a thrusting, successful society which was expanding fast and could expect to do so for the foreseeable future.

Many such schools survived into the nineteen-fifties and a few are still extant. The type was developed by the Victorians. Daily assembly in chapel or, failing that, in a school hall, preparation for leadership in society through prefectorial office, strict discipline, stern punishments, gaudy coats, cups, prizes and rewards—have not these been for most of us quite recently the signs of a good school? Yet all reflect the ideas of another age and would prepare our children for the past rather than for the future.

As the Church of England still bears some imprint of the sixteenth century and Methodism of the eighteenth, so this sort of school maintains the assumptions of the later nineteenth. That age held, for example, that education was for an élite, that we should keep children in their place and the sexes apart for as long as possible, that outdoor sport was next to godliness, that this world, like the next, should be well provided with rewards and punishments, that both the cane and the public

2

examination were expressions of society and of an ideal of incorruptible justice.

In the seventy years which have seen our country shaken to its foundations by two world wars, the imperial rôle abandoned, rural superseded by urban life, almost every facet of living revolutionised by scientific discovery and almost all established ideas upset, perhaps any surviving institution is bound to look old-fashioned. And the trouble with schools is that they last too long. This is even more true of ideas than it is of buildings. It is easy to reject the model described in an earlier paragraph, much less so to replace it. But if we had the opportunity, as at Egremont, of starting a new school in the middle sixties, how many of the traditional features ought we to retain?

The society for which we are preparing our children is no longer a hierarchy. The rôle of the school in it should not be divisive. Admittedly, it is not possible to have all the circumstances we should like in constructing a school system. But if we had them? The school should unite the district. It should include brothers and sisters, rich and poor, children of differing ability and any variety of talents—just as they come in families. And it should prepare its members for the community by being itself a part of it. In this too it will break with the English tradition.

For centuries the school has been separate, in fact and in intention. It may have begun in the cloisters. Religion, whether monastic or puritan, kept it apart from the world. For some people education has been a source of power, for others of culture. The symbol of the one may be the mediaeval castle, of the other perhaps the Palladian mansion. In either case the essential feature is that of separation from the multitude. The residential school (the particular product of the nineteenth century) has continued the tradition. The early elementary schools of our cities, if they had little else traditional about them, at least adhered to that one: they stood apart because they resembled nothing so much as a barrack or a gaol. Finally, the developing secondary schools of the twentieth century, accepting too readily the importance of team games, have been sited, wherever possible, with fields around them. This has its advantages, but it separates school and community.

3

In complete contrast was the planning by Cumberland of Wyndham School. As a large project, coeducational and comprehensive, it cost about £3 per head for every man, woman and child in the county. How ridiculous if it had been used only in the day time, the working week and the school term. It is in fact, and under the same management, a centre of further education (in which many of the day-time staff both teach and learn). It is a community centre in which more people are found in affiliated societies than as members of evening classes. It has its own Youth Centre on the premises, used in the morning for a Nursery Play Group and at lunch time for the recreation of teen-age pupils. The library is a building belonging half to the school and half to the public, with a reference room in its centre which is common ground. The very fine indoor swimming pool belongs to the public when the school is not in session. So does the playing field. Both are administered by a Committee, on which the headmaster sits, representative of both Education Authority and Rural District Council. The amenities were in fact provided by a joint effort of these bodies, to the great advantage of both

Thus on only a few days in the year (not even every Bank Holiday) is some part at least of the premises not officially in use by the community. Indeed, in one sense they are always in use: their open spaces are a playground for the young, garden seats make resting places for the elderly, the paths short-cuts for the housewife with her shopping basket or her pram. Where walls exist, they are so low as to offer rather a challenge than a barrier. The result is some loss to dignity but clearly a gain to the public good. In a sense, the building represents a return to the mediaeval church—a meeting place for the whole community.

Separateness, exclusiveness and some prestige have gone by the board. We teach as if in a goldfish bowl—and anything that goes wrong is quickly obvious to the public! To teachers with a traditional training this may sound very unattractive. The young accept with pleasure that the place belongs to the community. Extensive use has also proved that if people—even a community which was earlier based on mining and in the thirties was a distressed area—are offered the use of good

4

facilities, they will treat them well. In such a setting conventional ideas are bound to come under close scrutiny. When the setting and the imaginative nature of the plan have combined to attract an outstanding staff, many of them very young, it is to be expected that new concepts will emerge.

Here are a few of them. If a child of eleven is utterly different from a young man or woman of eighteen, they should not both be subject to the same régime. If their physical strength is vastly different, they should not have the same length of teaching week. They should certainly not meet together as an audience, for this is to place an impossible burden on any speaker. If the growth in them of moral attitudes is important, these are unlikely to be learned by overt propaganda but may gradually be acquired through friendly personal contact with more mature people. If that is true, then any striking of a child by a teacher represents a defeat, not a victory, for the power of good (even, in a trite and narrow phrase, for law and order). If all children have some talents, and these nearly always flourish under encouragement, hardly ever under disapproval, a system of competition must be wasteful of talent. That is the philosophy of our comprehensive school. Later chapters will study some expressions of it.

Wyndham offers an additional point of peculiarity. Its premises were designed as an exercise in decentralisation. If they have been used as was intended, much authority should be delegated. In fact, heads of sub-units (Houses and 'Sixth Form College') are expected to take many actions and decisions that might elsewhere belong to a headmaster. But a Wyndham pupil of eleven might be forgiven if he could not say where his school was. He cannot be in doubt about his House (see Chapter 4) but 'Wyndham' might mean to him nothing more precise or localised than 'Cambridge' does to its average student. For the school has no place where large numbers can meet: it is not intended to assemble them together. This is an obvious piece of economy. There can be few worse ways of spending £25,000 than in providing a hall which does duty very badly as a theatre, a dining hall or a gymnasium and, unless it does serve in these ways, is used only for a few minutes daily—for a function which is not appropriate to a large compre-

5

hensive school. But bricks and mortar (or even the willed absence of them) can express a philosophy. This omission does so.

The view implicit in the premises and (we hope) now explicit has these facets: The institution is not the focus of our thoughts. We wish to serve not it but ideals which are higher, if vaguer. If it develops a tradition, we do not wish to see this solidify (still less, ossify) into any outward or material expression. We deprecate a centralised direction with the headmaster daily 'on the bridge' or even 'in the pulpit'. Our most characteristic festivity is not a Speech Day (we do not like formalism, which for the young is either meaningless or abhorrent, and we do not award prizes) but a Summer Fair when several thousand people of all ages throng the premises. Finally, we have no desire to see any association specifically confined to former pupils. If our school means anything to them, it is best that they should feel this for themselves. Our only attempt to introduce a focal point for thinking is not obtrusive. It is found in the central block where everyone must often pass, though he need seldom linger.

As the visitor enters this area, he sees on the wall a stone legend. It begins by quoting the first sentence of the American Declaration of Independence ('We hold these truths to be self-evident, that all men are created equal, etc.') and goes on:

This school is dedicated to the brotherhood of all men and the infinite possibilities of the spirit which is in them, to freedom both from oppression and from prejudice, to the open mind and to the open door. On the wall appear names of men and women of our time who have championed one or other of these causes.

A list of about twenty names is steadily growing. It includes Mohandas Gandhi, Albert Schweitzer, Pope John XXIII, John Kennedy, Dag Hammarskjöld, Albert Luthuli, Helen Keller, Martin Luther King, Gladys Aylward, and Bertrand Russell. As others are added we hope that its silent witness may have effect when we who caused it to be set up are no longer present.

One more aspect of the decentralised organisation concerns the growth of self-government. House Councils came quickly into being but for a long time it did not seem appropriate to

6

form a School Council when in so many ways the school did not function as a single unit. In particular, the 'Sixth Form College' (described in Chapter 9) was always intended to be virtually independent. The growth in 1969 of the Reception House was a further step, however logical in itself, away from centralisation. Tentatively, we introduced Year meetings and committees, conscious that their 'horizontal' structure conflicted in a sense with the 'vertical' arrangement of the Houses. Having found that they fulfil a useful role, we began a School Council in the term when these words were written. True, we were not yet seven years old. But many others have proceeded much faster in this respect. Our relative slowness reflects a view about radical ideas. They are always welcome. When a new institution is to be formed, they should positively be sought out. As it develops its own vitality, new concepts should still be looked for, particularly as an antidote to the growth of routine. But, so far as possible, they should represent a development rather than a destruction of the existing nucleus, and their introduction should be gradually prepared.

NOTES

1 These words were written before the Skinheads arrived on the scene. Their fashion weakens the particular, but not the general application of the thought.

Chapter Two

What is the purpose of a school?

This searching question must lie somewhere in the mind of any thinking headmaster, though it is of the kind which we usually succeed in keeping in the background. In a sense, the actions of any Head, however constricted or driven by immediate circumstances, express his answer, just as his conduct as a man establishes whether he believes in God—or rather, what kind o ultimate authority or values he does believe in. But we are not asked this kind of question when we are appointed and may easily be too busy in our normal routine to face it. Indeed, so much of our preoccupation (especially in a large secondary school) will be with the obvious purposes—to help pupils to obtain qualifications, to guide the choice of careers, to harmonise the elements of the organisation—that we have some excuse if we seldom consider any larger or transcendent aim. Does it or should it exist?

Perhaps we can go no further than the general: the aim of any school is to be as good as it can be. This still leaves us to define 'good'. And to do the best it can for all its pupils? If we add this, we have already begun to define. For it would have been accepted at one time that a secondary school was very good if it regularly sent a fair number of pupils to universities and won most of its athletic fixtures. According to the only visible criteria, it was competing successfully with other schools —and it might be tedious to inquire whether they were all competing on equal terms. By now we can see this judgement as inadequate. For the outward signs mentioned above could co-exist with a neglect of the interests, needs and abilities of very many of the pupils—of all, in fact, whose proven shortcomings made them unable to take part in the competitions or had caused them to be eliminated early. Today we can see that we are charged with the welfare of all our pupils. We have recognised that it is their individual interests, rather than those of the school as an institution, which should be our chief concern. And this becomes even more obvious as our schools cease to be selective.

If that general objective—to do our best for every pupil—is accepted, the particular aims of any school must be chosen in relation to its circumstances. They will differ as between an Infants', an Approved and Manchester Grammar School. But if we confine ourselves to maintained secondary schools, some generalisation may be possible.

There is to some extent an English view of the question. That a school is first a community and only secondly a place of learning is an idea widely held in our country. Most continental (though not American) practice would reverse the priority. Our view was formed in the last century. In part it must be due to a positive fear of intellectualism ingrained by events in the minds of our then leaders. A generation of these had stood almost alone against Napoleon after watching the French *Ancien Régime* first undermined, as they thought, by intellectuals, then overthrown by terrorists. Their descendants saw Europe shaken by the convulsions of 1848 and noted how large a part in them was played by students. (The parallel with 1968 is close.) This fear of the questioning mind was supported by the great success of residential schools in moulding gentlemen, not a few being the first their family had produced. The factors combined to establish the view that character was more important than intellect.

The Public Schools were undoubtedly successful. They catered for a group which was ready to conform; they could refer to a widely held code of beliefs and, to some extent, of ethics; they were borne up on the rising tides of nationalism and of national triumph. Thus collective virtues took precedence over individual ones and stoicism over sensitivity. Even in the schools later set up for other classes the same ideals could be invoked, all the more readily if a chief aim of these schools was to strengthen society by keeping everybody in the station to which God had called him.

Today the position is utterly different. By contrast with a

9

century ago, 1972 in England seems a time of relative anarchy
—though not indeed, relatively, of violence. We have shed our
Empire and our position as the world's policeman, our
theology and our agreed values, our former concept of nationalism and, perhaps, our views on race and colour. Have we
sufficiently revised our view of the school and its function?

If we have not, the school will still appear as an authoritarian
place. Its function will be to dispense what J. K. Galbraith has
called 'the conventional wisdom' and to make it acceptable to
the young. Is it time that this rôle was abandoned?

The answer is not simple. It is natural to argue that in a world
of uncertainty the school should represent the stable environment and the unchanging beliefs. But if the beliefs have been
shaken, what value can there be in presenting them as still
firm? Indeed, perhaps the most general, and the most justified,
indictment of school in the recollection of many adults is that
it represented a time of unreality, not necessarily of unhappi-
ness, but out of touch with life as it is lived. The teacher is
almost by definition less than a man, his sphere narrower than
that of others. If this is what the school has achieved through
seeking to be unspotted from the world, it would seem to have
attempted the wrong task. No wonder if it has not succeeded.

To some extent, of course, the school's dilemma is that of
every parent. The young child in his innocence 'cannot bear
very much reality' and, just as he is not allowed to play with his
father's razor, he can hardly handle without damage some of
the ideas which are commonplace among adults. Or so it would
seem. We cannot prove that to be sheltered from harsh ideas
(sex, death, speculation on moral, religious or political issues)
is really good for children. In a primitive tribe, or in a present-
day slum, there is probably no such sheltering and it cannot be
shown beyond doubt that this has done harm.

Here is a clear argument against over-long continuation in
any single stage of organised education. If—and the doubt
remains—it is right to shelter the infant from adult ideas, this is
not proper treatment for an older child. If we must temper our
views for the ears of eleven year olds, it is almost evidently
unwise to do so for the adolescent about to enter the world of
wage-earning—and the younger he does so, the more likely he

10

is to find himself on the factory floor rather than in the more restrained atmosphere of the clerical office.

If a secondary school is to include pupils of eleven and others of eighteen (and the wisdom of this too must come in question), it must treat them very differently. Even with the younger ones, it is doubtful how long the concept of a school as a day nursery can hold good. For the older pupils cannot be prevented from having friends, including brothers and sisters, among the younger. They come from the same homes. Their parents or relatives, television, the Press, the street, the park, the youth centre and other influences combine to break down barriers and create One World. We are forced to the conclusion that, while the younger child will often be kept by sheer lack of interest from close involvement with the adult world, we can never count on this. As with the children of our own families, we live among them and we must be prepared to answer their questions.

'To answer their questions.' Is this what a school is for? The view seems tenable that if it did this, and did it with full candour, it would have achieved a great deal. Certainly a school ought to be a place in which it is natural to ask questions. A place in which answers are given frankly. A place in which the answer 'I don't know' is given with equally ready frankness. For this last answer, spoken not with impatience but with regret, has special value. It subsumes a number of ideas— that knowledge is boundless and the adventure of seeking it unending; that the teacher is a fellow seeker rather than the mouthpiece of truth; that the pupil has his place in the search and is neither an inferior creature nor, in the old-fashioned sense, one 'under authority'. It glimpses the kind of world for which the school should be a preparation.

It would be simplistic to say that the schools of 1870 were set up to confirm authority, while those of today set out to question it—but it would be partly true. If we had to choose between unquestioned dogma and uncontrolled individual judgement—the problem of the Reformation—we should, however reluctantly, opt for the second. The first way cannot be right, the second might conceivably lead to truth. Certainly we do not want our schools to produce conformists, to 'turn

out a type' (even a 'good' one) or to be run on the principle—
'because I say so'. In our own eyes and hence in stark fact, we
do not hold an authority which is to be exercised without the
consent of the governed.

A world of petty rules, some based merely on tradition and
others on regimentation, enforced by an authority which is, in
the last resort, arbitrary and self-perpetuating, which may, if it
likes, appeal to force as its sanction—this has been a justified
description of many schools in the past. It should not be recog-
nisable today. Such a school prepared for a different sort of
society. Both are now obsolete. We grope our way as yet
towards democracy and are far from sure how to interpret the
concept in school. But at least we grope. And we sense that
prefects and canes do not represent the means of finding it.

But there is a further sense in which 'the school as a community' is to be re-interpreted today. More and more we begin
to see schools as a part, and not an isolated part, of the adult
world. In many a small town the secondary (just as in many a
village the primary) school is the chief public building. Mere
common sense suggests that so expensive a creation should be
used by the community as much as possible. The realisation
that education does not finish with schooldays will increasingly
bring the adults to the building in the evening. And more and
more we recognise that the school cannot, indeed should not,
fight the parents and the home for the soul of the child. It was
only in the residential school that such an undertaking could
seem feasible. Home and school must try to work together. The
parents cannot help in the child's education if they have no
contact with it. The school cannot educate the child fully in
ignorance of his home background. And though some parents
may wish to oppose the school, they will do so only the more
bitterly if they feel unwelcome in it.

It seems we have rejected the closed, authoritarian idea of the
school. We no longer seek an isolated community but wish to
mingle freely with the life of the neighbourhood. Do we then
accept the standards of the market-place? Is there to be no
'cradle of security', no moral training in the school we are
trying to create?

Yes, indeed there is or should be. But it will consist of

12

principles rather than precepts. Effective training of this kind will seldom be overt. The mere fact that some schools in our country are multi-racial while almost all have members with varieties of religious belief, including none, makes it impossible to appeal to a common creed or even to a common code of ethics. And when Keats said, 'We hate poetry which has a palpable design upon us', he spoke for more than poetry. Whether or not direct preaching was ever effective in guiding the conduct of young people, it does not seem to be so today. Yet there is no need to despair.

Teachers are, in the experience of the writer, good people.[1] If very little agreement on dogma can be found among them, the fundamental tenet, 'God is love', broadly interpreted and unconnected with any creed, is almost universally honoured. The spirit of our time would add, 'All men are brothers'. This too finds ready acceptance. Despite all the criticism of the present young generation for slack standards and selfishness, they are the first to have responded widely to the call for voluntary service. In the face of what they have done and are doing, in school, at home and abroad, it is impossible to say that we have no basis on which to build. From such agreement can be evolved a community where the human being is valued and consideration for others assumed. If we refrain from trying to preach more than we believe, if we confine our preaching for the most part to the expression through action of these great ideas, it is still possible to create of a school a place of moral training as our forefathers wished.

NOTES

1   This view is based on meeting, as H.M.I., an unusual number of them.

Chapter Three

Children and their potential

What proportion of the country's children should go to university? Or be selected at eleven—if selection obtains? Or be expected to stay to the Sixth Form? Or be classified as educationally sub-normal? Precise answers to all these questions have been asserted and even forcefully defended in recent years. But mistakenly. The crux of the current argument about education is that answers to such questions, if they exist at all, exist only for particular groups and areas. Even so, they are always changing. And although there is a possible minor variant in the difference of standards set up by succeeding generations, the truth is that the human race does not know what it can do until it tries.

'More means worse.' The phrase, whether or not correctly attributed to Mr Amis, has had wide currency in the Sixties. A little earlier, in 1954, Roger Bannister ran the first four-minute mile. Before he did so, expert judges had debated for years, and some had doubted, whether the feat would ever be achieved by man. Within a dozen years it had been repeated on three hundred occasions, the time of four minutes had become commonplace for leading athletes and the record had been lowered by the time equivalent of some seventy yards. Within the same period in Cumberland the award of Major Scholarships to university (based on a constant criterion of two Grade 'A' passes at the Advanced level of the General Certificate of Education) had gone up from nine in 1957 to forty ten years later.

These facts are either common knowledge or easily verifiable. They support the view that the limits of human potential cannot be defined. In intellectual no less than in physical terms, what an individual or a group may achieve cannot be forecast without reference to the circumstances. And while there is considerable variation in the natural ability of children, their achievement in school tends to be very strongly influenced by whatever is expected of them. It is likely that most children achieve less, and many much less, than they might. The greatest single factor in this shortcoming is the lack of belief on the part of their teachers, or of society, that they had such potential.

It is this conviction which for many of us constitutes the indictment of a selective system of secondary education. For in selecting a fifth or a quarter of the age-group (the proportion varying greatly in different parts of the country and usually bearing a closer relation to the past history than to the present nature of the district), the system has been rejective of the vast majority. In so far as these children were labelled intellectually inferior, they began their secondary school career under a crippling handicap. They were then, for the most part, taught in larger classes, often in inferior buildings, usually by less well qualified staff and always with more limited expectations than the minority who had been selected. The fact that a tiny proportion managed to overcome these handicaps did not constitute the redress of an unjust and wasteful system. It merely indicated, because the numbers were so small, that the original assessment amounted, in the conditions, to a self-fulfilling prophecy.

Today the injustice has been so widely recognised that it need not be laboured here. The rest of this chapter will concentrate on facts. From the limited experience of one school in a very few years it will adduce evidence of what happens to the child as soon as the handicaps are removed.

Wyndham School was formed as a comprehensive in 1964. It consisted then of four 'years' only. Its First Form included the whole of the age group in the area except for about a dozen children whose parents had removed them to schools at a distance. All pupils older than eleven had spent one or more years in other secondary schools or in the unreorganised top of an 'all-age' village school. These tops were absorbed into the new school. Otherwise transfer to Wyndham above the age of eleven was voluntary and, very naturally, less favoured if the child had been for some time in another school, still less if he or she was enjoying success there. In consequence, the school had a structure tapering towards the top both in numbers and in intellectual ability. The composition was as set out below.

Year	Roll	Composition	Year of taking 11+ selection test
I	210	Whole age-group (less about 12)	1964 (resulting 'order' notified in confidence to Wyndham School but *not* to the pupils)
II	200	Whole age-group less an uncertain number (possibly 20–30) who had chosen to remain in selective schools. Includes 45 previously 'selected' and now choosing transfer	1963 (the majority) but about 15 pupils had been rejected in 1962, then admitted in 1963 to selective schools as 'over-age late developers'
III	150	31 pupils originally 'selected', about half of them already rather unsuccessful in the selective school	1962
IV	100	About a dozen pupils originally 'selected', none having been successful in the selective school	1961

These 'years' have been supplemented by a few later transfers or new arrivals in the area as well as depleted by migration. The school's 'Sixth Form College' was opened, independently of the rest of the pupils, in 1965 by voluntary transfer of twenty-five pupils from Fifth Forms elsewhere. Thus the first entrants to higher education actually left Wyndham in 1967, but none of these had been a member of the school below the Sixth. It is with the careers of younger pupils that this analysis is concerned. The many imponderable qualities which a pupil may bring to or derive from a school are not here in question. For this particular purpose it is not relevant that many were delightful pupils and have since made excellent employees. We are concerned only with a review, in the light of events, of the verdict passed on the great majority, in 1961, 1962 or 1963, that they did not have the potential for an academic education. We shall also consider, though their school career is not yet completed,[2] the academic progress of year groups who never underwent the process of rejection.[1]

Of the 1961 group, our original Fourth, the few who had been selected had not been successful in their selective schools. Although these pupils, arriving so late, did not produce any great academic achievements, two who went, after 'A' level, to Colleges of Education commented that, had they remained at their previous school, they would certainly have left at sixteen because they felt themselves failures there. Another girl, who had three years of 'rejection' before she came to Wyndham, also went to a College of Education with three 'A' level passes.

The 1962 group had of course also mostly been rejected at 11 plus and had two years of restricted opportunity since then. Three of these rejects, however, went from Wyndham in 1969 to read for degrees (in, respectively, Physics, Economics and Architecture). A fourth did so in 1970—a still more remarkable feat because at the Fifth Form stage she had shown no more than earnest endeavour and gained only a single pass in GCE.

The 'class of 1963' made our original Second Form. All had spent a year elsewhere since taking the 11 plus test and some forty-five, out of two hundred, had been selected. This number included fifteen who, having been rejected in 1962, had been allowed a year later to re-start the secondary course as later selections. Because they had already been segregated, in their curriculum as well as in their classes, it seemed impossible not to keep them so in the new school. But forty-five children could not be taught as two complete forms—we do not have that kind of staffing! Diffidently we included a number of others (rejects of 1963) with them. After a few months we added others, later still more. Thus when the 'year' came to take its first public examinations, in 1968, the informed eye could distinguish numerous educational strata among them. There were the '1963 successful', the '1962 late entry', who had joined them, the group of 1963 rejects who had been put to work with the selected, later additions and still later. Only the first two strata could be said to have had five years of secondary education. The rest had had a makeshift year, mostly in all-age schools, before Wyndham opened, and then four with us. Yet all faced the same examinations.

17

The year as a whole did well. But the overall view of the strata yielded these general observations. If any group is selected or promoted, its morale will be raised. It will mainly do well. But, because these are human beings, in each such group there will be a minority, at least one pupil, who will make the exception. Each successive stratum had had a shorter and less satisfactory preparation for the examinations than the one above it. Yet each had its majority of success, its minority of disappointment. And still there emerged one or two pupils, passed over by every one of these selections or promotions, who came through at the end to surprise us with a good all-round result.

The 'class of 1964' were of course virtually the full age-group. They had taken the selection test but did not know its results (which remained confidential within the school files). However, our timid approach in that first year to the question of unstreaming (see Chapter 7) meant that, in effect, some sixty pupils had greater expectations overtly placed upon them than the rest. They therefore had an initial advantage of morale, although neither then nor at any later time did they have priority in staffing, educational resources or the size of class. After the first three years, almost all distinction of grouping within the year disappeared through the system of options. Only in the three compulsory subjects—english, mathematics and science—was setting retained and here the ablest sets suffered the handicap of being also the largest.

The examination results of this group (obtained in 1969) were bound to be interesting, if only because this was the last on which a verdict had been passed as to their potential at age eleven, even though it had not been publicised.[2] Some migration from the county (which chanced to hit this particular year harder than any before or since) reduced by 1969 the number of pupils who had theoretically been 'selected' five years earlier to fifty. Their results showed the usual variations, from a maximum of nine passes to a minimum of none (obtained by two boys who came to us after selection elsewhere). The average was 5.0. This was much as might have been expected (perhaps very slightly better), had the same group been given the selective education for which they had notionally qualified.

18

Attention now turns to those deemed inferior in 1964. Naturally in the year group there were some who left from the Fourth Form and many others who took no subject in GCE nor obtained any Grade 1 pass in CSE. But fifty-three pupils did obtain one or more of such successes. The best of them obtained eight, the weakest only one. The average for the group worked out at 3.2. This was perceptibly less than the score obtained by the former group. But by the definition of 1964, partly compounded by our own action in weakly accepting it, every single one of these pupils was less able, and some far less, than each of the former. It may be of interest that the boy who obtained eight passes was No 68, that is eighteen places below the pass line, in the 11 plus list (indeed, in the Third Form he had seemed to be an unsatisfactory pupil). The lowest in the list to obtain five passes was No 107. The last to obtain any pass in GCE was No 148 (who got two, including mathematics). And the lowest to obtain a Grade 1 in CSE was No 192, who achieved three of them and missed by the narrowest possible margin adding GCE passes in both physics and chemistry. It is worth remarking that Nos 68, 107 and 192 were all boys. For it is a frequent experience that the 11 plus test discriminates against them in favour of girls, for obvious reasons of physical maturity.

The experience recorded is of course very limited—to a single school even though to several hundred children. Its results, however, all point in the same direction. A child's academic prospects are very closely related to morale and this is directly affected by the attitude towards him of his teachers. There are geese as well as swans. But very many children might almost be said to await the word of adults to decide which shall be their category.

NOTES

1 The passage was composed in 1970.
2 The reference is to passes at 'O' level of GCE with the addition of Grade 1 passes in CSE.

Chapter Four

The child in the
large school

One of the most obvious features of our time is the increasing
size of our institutions. Nations grow, government departments increase in size as well as multiplying, firms, farms, universities and schools are similarly affected. A particular reason
with many people for distrusting the comprehensive movement
is that it produces large schools. Yet no such concern has been
expressed about the many famous schools which are also large.
A glance through a list of boys' schools in 1966 produced
immediately twenty-five well-known names of Public or
Grammar Schools with a roll of over 800. No fewer than
fourteen of them had over 1000. These included, of course,
Eton College and Manchester Grammar School. Evidently,
size alone does not ensure distrust. It is true that many comprehensives are much larger than this. But twenty years ago we
should have regarded a school of 800 as very large and one of
1000 as almost monstrous.

Simultaneously with this development—and not, it would
seem, merely as a corrective to it—has been found an increasing
sense of care and compassion for the individual. Voluntary
service at home and abroad, Shelter, Oxfam, War on Want,
Amnesty International—these movements do not simply exist;
they command wide support. In schools we have more and
more come to realise that it is not merely the group achievement, nor even the successes of some individuals within the
group, but the personal fulfilment and flowering of each child
which is to be aimed at. If we look back to the mass instruction
of a hundred children simultaneously—which could be seen in
the elementary schools of the past—and realise that out of this
has grown the sensitive handling of every child in even large
classes which has long been common in our best infant schools,

we are witnessing a miracle. This spirit has spread upwards to the junior schools. Individual or small group work in place of class instruction, abolition of streaming, open plan classrooms, a relaxed atmosphere from which the child strolls out at morning break, still talking absorbedly, instead of hurling himself through the doors of the authoritarian cage to rush up and down screaming until summoned back by the blast of a whistle—all these are signs of the advance towards the family concept of a school and away from the regimented institution. Already the turn has come of the secondary school.

In some ways the very large school of today, if it has the good fortune to be purpose-built, has the best prospect of avoiding depersonalisation. For it is forced to recognise that it is large and to do something about it. In the school which became established and successful when it was relatively small and has since expanded by degrees, there is a greater danger that the individual may be overlooked. Cherished traditions may be unhelpful in this respect if they include demands for conformity, a greater care for 'standards' than for free growth, and hierarchical attitudes. Not the least fault of these Spartan traits is that they make it appear easy to subdue and control large masses. So it is with armies. So perhaps it has to be. But so it should not be with a school. Here the need, especially for a child as young as eleven, is to break down the big community into acceptable units, to humanise, to achieve if possible the atmosphere of a family.

Wyndham School was planned about 1960. It had to cater for an unusual community, very mixed socially but containing a rather higher than average proportion of able children. This was due to the presence, as the chief source of employment in the area, of the atomic energy station at Windscale. Workers in technology, at very different levels of skill but including many graduates, figured largely among the parents of the prospective clientèle. But this large community, some of it recruited from outside the county, might change in character, expand, contract, or even disappear, according to decisions taken far away in the corridors of power. It was therefore realistic to provide a comprehensive school. This could more easily take account of fluctuations in the number or the intellectual calibre of the children to be taught than could separate schools for selective and non-selective children.

If there was to be a single secondary school for the area, it must be a large one, not perhaps by the standards of a city (the roll was not likely much to exceed 1500) but certainly in the eyes of West Cumberland. In the quiet villages lying between the fells and the Irish Sea heads were shaken over the inevitable and crushing impersonality of so large a school. Such fears were very understandable but they could be dispelled. Plans were laid to accomplish this.

The school was built as a collection of sub-units, none to be very large. Moreover, each was to cater for a restricted age-range so that younger children would be kept separate from those more than a few years older. In the beginning, when the school was formed with fewer than 700 children and only four 'years' (11–15), eight purpose-built Houses divided the community into vertical and 'comprehensive' sections. When the Sixth Form came into being, it occupied separate accommodation, designed as a students' union with the emphasis on preparing for adult life and higher education. Then, after five years with the school fully developed in structure though not yet at full size (the roll was about 1200), there was implemented a plan deferred from the original blue-print—a new Reception House, to take all children for their first year, aiming at a 'post-primary' atmosphere, bridging the gap between homely primary and over-organised secondary education, and deferring by a year the entry to a senior House.

By this last means the eight senior Houses reverted to catering for four years only, the age-groups 12–16. They lost at a stroke both the charm of children fresh to secondary education and most of the daily problems which seem very large to the child concerned but to nobody else. They could gear themselves to dealing with the problems of adolescence, both those of educational and career guidance and those of discipline—which so often appear serious to everybody except the person at the centre of them.

No organisation can be perfect. Wyndham's is easily faulted. It would be foolish to deny this or to suggest that others should necessarily copy our system. What seems more constructive is

22

to look at the principles which we have tried to follow and some of the methods used, as possibly of interest and capable of adaptation to different conditions elsewhere.

Three principles are accepted. First, that every child must be known, and well known, to his Head of House. It is likely that at least one of the House staff will also be concerned with him as, in any case of importance, will also be the headmaster. But nothing can replace the Head of House as the teacher with the personality, the discretion and the influence in school to see any problem through. (The size of senior Houses does not exceed 140. As Sixth Form and Reception House are larger than this, rather different arrangements apply with more de-centralised care.)

Second, that a problem which is important to the child is also important to us. It may be only a lost book. It may be illness or a broken home. We should be aware of and ready to help in it.

Third, it is essential that we know the parents. They learn early the habit of coming to school and regular evenings are held, by year-groups, for discussion of progress. On such occasions records show that attendance may be as high as ninety or as low as fifty per cent. They are not therefore sufficient. It is the duty of the Head of House to meet the parents and to know the home. Unless they come to us, he (or she) goes to them. It is the accepted thing that, if a problem has arisen in school, 'I'll drop in and see the parents this evening'.

How does the Head of House get to know his children? He meets them before they enter the House but his greatest asset is possession of his own identifiable section of the school premises. Here the members of the House register, keep their belongings, meet for daily assembly and notices, dine, talk with their friends, stay if they wish for recreation after school. Before the school opened, some voices assured us that Houses in a day school would never mean more than units for competition in sport. As it happened, it was many weeks after the start before our premises were sufficiently completed for any inter-House sport to be played. But within one week their physical presence as a community which lived and ate together, allied to the care of their staff, had made each of the Houses into an entity, self-conscious in the best sense. This has continued ever since,

23

despite the fact that inter-House competition is very slightly regarded. It does not seem to us that the value of a family as a human relationship is attested by its seeking to outdo its neighbours in sport or anything else.

The House tries to reproduce the family, with all the emphasis which would be placed there on the differences between individuals rather than on their conforming to a pattern set. It is assisted by a school policy which does not admit canes and which says that the essential in dealing with any child is to know as much as possible about him. (All are called by their first names at all times. For the first five years of the school's life every child and every teacher wore a lapel badge with his name on it, though we eventually decided that replacement was becoming too expensive.) How far can this emphasis on the personal enable staff to dispense with administrative records?

A child's record from his primary school, a very simple one, precedes him and is kept by the House. In the school office exists a record card of our own complete with his photograph. Both school office and House maintain a file for each child. This is the more necessary because correspondence with the home is most often done by the headmaster, with a copy for the House, simply to make best use of secretarial facilities. Meanwhile, the school record with most detail of a child is being built up in the form of his school report. This is cumulative by subjects with a separate sheet for each held in a folder. The summaries are written not by a form teacher but, at considerable length, by Head of House with an addition by Head or Deputy Head of School.

Some Heads of House feel that all this is still insufficient. Much else, of course, happens in a child's school life which is notable but not covered by the system as outlined above. Particularly important are interviews with him and with his parents. Heads of House decide for themselves how much should be recorded. Our policy is that each is free to make his own system and that no administrative records are valuable in themselves (it is the use made of them which has value) or should be allowed to become a substitute for action. Few families keep written records about their own children. If the pupil is a person of importance to his Head of House, the latter

24

will supplement the basic records by a store of knowledge carried in his head. And he will share much of it with his Deputy, a person of opposite sex, who carries with him the care of all the boys and girls. She (or he) and the other members of the House staff make a team. If or when the Head of House moves to promotion, they can all supplement the detailed hand-over of his responsibilities.

The composition of the House is comprehensive. It should include all the members of any one family in the school. Occasional exceptions to this practice are made because every child, before entering, is invited to name a friend with whom he wishes to be placed. Such a one can mean more to him than a brother or sister several years older. And there is also a 'locality link' in the case of small villages. Those which send us no more than half a dozen children a year have an affiliation to a particular House so that all join without ever being so numerous as to swamp it. By contrast, the larger primary schools are deliberately spread over many Houses, to prevent the growth of cliques.

With us there is a further function to be played by the House in relation to social engineering. Because ours is a rural area and remote geographically from the stream of national life, the inter-village feud has survived longer here than in many parts of Britain. Irish immigration in the nineteenth century gave us a large Roman Catholic minority. Less than fifty years ago religious rivalries were pursued in frequent fighting. Only in the last ten have they ceased to be bitter, and this is still not true of all adherents. And we have one additional source of discord.

This is the presence in this ancient rural and mining area of the atomic energy plant and the scientists' dormitory of Sea-scale. The little town is lively, given over to one occupation, almost entirely middle class, largely immigrant to Cumberland. Here are the ingredients for yet another feud. It can often be seen in action. A function of Wyndham is to dissolve it. The school could not claim more, at the moment of writing, than that there is less discord than there would be without its existence. But consider these facts. The Roman Catholic families send their children voluntarily to Wyndham. Their Church has come not only to accept this but to approve specifically of their attending the lessons of religious education. And since the first term, every Tuesday has seen the presence at our House assemblies (which all children attend) of seven clergymen, representing all three major denominations, who take the assembly in seven Houses on a rota and in perfect harmony. Of course this owes more to Pope John XXIII than it does to Wyndham. But if it can happen despite a hundred years of bitterness, the far more recent 'quarrel' can also be resolved. We believe that the House communities, by deliberate mixing of the parties, will bring this about.

Here, to repeat, is no blue-print for others. The principle of sub-division in the interests of the child is of key importance. So, it would seem, is close knowedge of him by someone able to exercise immediate influence in the school. We recognise that this style of care, like the Welfare State, may be abused. Some children will ask for too much. It is also exceptionally exacting for teachers. Since House premises are the 'homes' of the children and all are free to use them at all break-times, the staff may spend the whole day in quite close contact with the pupils. Finally, this emphasis on the pastoral carries an inherent danger of a clash with academic interests exercised by other teachers. Given two different structures within the school, of the Houses and the Departments, each concerned with the same children, the seeds of a power-struggle are present. In the early years of the school it could be discerned in embryo. The only way to avoid it is to appoint Heads of Houses who see clearly the importance of academic aims and Heads of Department who care deeply about the welfare of the child. This Wyndham has been lucky enough to do. The two join hands on numerous occasions, most obviously when at the Third Year stage it is necessary for both to advise child and parent over the choice of options to be taken in the Fourth and Fifth Forms.

If the form, as the unit of teaching, can be a part of the House organisation, this should lessen the danger of a clash. Only by a movement towards 'unstreaming' can it be achieved (see Chapter 7), if there is to be an approximate balance of ability in the composition of Houses.

Is there room for the outside advice of an expert beyond the

Head of House? We make use of this for all children in the Careers Master because, although he works closely with Heads of Houses, it seems too much to expect that his expertise, kept up to date by collaboration with the Ministry of Labour, by reading and by attendance at conferences, could be paralleled among many colleagues. Similarly, the child with special difficulties of temperament, ability or circumstances is discussed with Children's Officer and Educational Psychologist. Both are regular visitors. Is there a case for the appointment to the staff of a virtually full-time Counsellor?

Some schools and some Authorities make good use of these specially trained teachers. Such an appointment can obviously be of great value. He or she may have the advantage of not being involved with the child in any relationship of authority—though School Counsellors have been heard to say that their position is weakened *vis à vis* both teachers and pupils if they do not carry the responsibility of teaching. If the school's régime is authoritarian it is obviously hard for any teacher to be seen in the rôle of counsellor. This in itself would constitute an argument against authoritarianism. For an effective system of pastoral care must surely depend on many, preferably on all, members of the staff. It is not a 'subject' which can be left to a single person, however expert. Neither can the presence of even several experts achieve the aim from which we started, of breaking down the mass of the large school into units where the individual can feel at home. Whatever system of sub-division is most appropriate to a particular school, something of the sort is essential. And for a school to be large enough to need sub-dividing in this way, it probably needs only to have a few hundred pupils.

As a final word, what about continuity? In the past it has been taken for granted that this was an infinitely valuable element in education. (Perhaps here too the influence of the monastery was felt.) Clearly, it has benefits. But, like other good things, it can be had in too large supply. Seven years is too long a period to hold the child—who in the course of it ceases to be a child—under the same régime. The separate development of our 'Sixth Form College' (see Chapter 9) seems now almost not to need defending, at least so far as its social aspects

27

alone are concerned. The principle of 'limited continuity' is increasingly recognized by the growth of Middle Schools and indeed has always characterised the independent sector of education. The fact is that our maintained secondary schools originally existed as in effect 11–16 schools and grew tiny Sixth Forms almost as an after-thought. Today these are too large to exist as mere appendages.

Have we gone too far at Wyndham in having three stages— the Reception House, the Senior House and the 'Sixth Form College'? The one most open to question seems the single-year span of the first.[1] Indeed in the five years before it was opened, we were consistently sceptical of the value of so short a period. We actually devised in 1968 a plan for creating instead Junior Houses to take the first two years and Senior Houses for the next three: it was only on detailed considerations of how to deploy personnel and plant, not on any general principle, that it was finally given up. But, before leaving the subject, let us remember how different is the time-scale of a young child from our own. In our sight his whole school career passes quite quickly. To him the end of a year (and especially the first) must seem in September beyond human vision. This should weigh with us in planning for him.

NOTES

1   For further discussion of this subject see Chapter 14, 'Towards flexibility: objectives'.

Chapter Five

The school and
the home

'Do you like it this way? Doesn't it give a lot of trouble?' These
questions have been asked by very many visitors to the community school of shared facilities which was described in
Chapter 1. The answer to both is 'Yes'. Without doubt it would
be easier to have the premises locked up as soon as the school
had finished with them (although ours have no perimeter
which could be closed). It would also be easier to control the
pupils, in the most limited sense of 'control', if there were canes
to use upon them. And it would be easier to organise their
education without making personal contact with their parents.

Or would it? Certainly many difficulties would be saved.
They include: the eight to ten evenings spent by many staff in
each school year in discussing work with one or other of the
seven year-groups which compose an 11–18 school; the fort-
night (including each evening) devoted in February to advising
all Fifth Formers, together with their parents, on career and
Sixth Form prospects; the days given similarly to Fourth
Form leavers; the days of interviews which follow GCE results
in late August; and hundreds of individual interviews during
the year. These arise from consulting parents over all matters of
importance—those which affect every child, like choice of
course, those touching particular groups, like an excursion to
the Continent, and those concerned only with individuals, like
a serious lapse of attitude to work or in conduct, a complaint,
an injury, a change of form or a nervous crisis (in a school of
1200 one or other of these vicissitudes will occur every week).
If parents were not considered, we should not visit their homes
nor write to them about their children's problems. We should
not send them circulars about school events nor invite them to
functions. We might feel free to sum up a child's work for the

term with a laconic 'Lazy', instead of spending time over a more detailed and constructive comment. We should not be worried by complaints about the shortcomings of ourselves, our organisation or the fellow pupils of the complainant's child—but our life as teachers would be the poorer. Our pupils would be less well educated. And we should lose the delight of an occasional tribute from a grateful parent.

The community school stands for shared facilities. A modern philosophy of education sees the care of the child as shared between parent and teacher, to the advantage (in the ultimate sense) of all three.

One of the saddest minor episodes at Wyndham was the arrival on the second day of a term of an eleven-year-old boy alone and provided with nothing but his birth certificate. It is important to bear steadily in mind the good which is envisaged because there are inevitably problems of communication between ourselves and many parents.

We are concerned with the same child but we do not always see him from the same angle. Nor, if we have the same view of him and his powers, do we necessarily agree on general educational principles nor on his particular needs. Very few parents today lack interest in their child's education—at least until the time when he has been shown to have lost interest himself. But, very understandably, some are diffident when it comes to talking over the alarming technicalities of work which they themselves have never encountered or have long forgotten. There is seldom any difficulty in obtaining the parent's attendance when it is for discussion with a single, already known and trusted teacher, usually the Head of House. A particular advantage of such interviews is that they can be programmed so that the parent loses little or no time in waiting for his appointment.

The best way to a good contact, we have found, lies in a personal appointment with the Head of House at the end of a child's first term. A considerable number of parents will have attended the pre-school entry meeting in the previous June but now for the first time the Head of House not only knows the child well himself but has a report to hand from all his teachers. The time is also good because the parent has not lost the

30

initial hopefulness and spirit of co-operation usually given to a new school. (If there has been any crisis during the term to affect the child, probably parent and Head of House have already met, but this would be the exception.) For occasions such as these we have registered as high as ninety per cent of a House roll and should be very dissatisfied with less than three-quarters. This leaves only a few to be seen by special appointment. Much lower figures, however, are recorded at the 'Year meetings' for discussion of work with all teachers concerned.

At such meetings our records show a remarkable correlation between the attendance of the parent and the child's apparent success in school (measured by whether he is in a 'quicker' or a 'slower' form). This constitutes an argument in itself for 'unstreaming' (to be discussed in Chapter 7). When we had our forms arranged in three 'blocks', the highest rate of attendance was shown for the top group. When we merged the second group with the first, we found that the parents of these children also registered a 'strong form' attendance!

Statistics of this sort are always worth keeping. A further question has been thrown up by ours: which parents stay away? By the Fourth and Fifth Form stages it is no longer always the one whose child is doing badly. The increasing complication of the work frightens off the less educated parent. He may fear (without justification) that he is going to be asked to rehearse his child's irregular verbs! We have attempted to solve the problem by offering as alternatives a general, necessarily less detailed, interview with the familiar Head of House and a series of talks with the subject teachers. We know that the educated parent will choose the latter and the less sophisticated the former, but discretion obviously demands that we leave the option open.

There are, of course, middle-class parents who take no interest in their children's education, but they are rare. Less uncommon is the one who takes too close an interest—in one of several ways. One consists in overestimating his child's ability, another in making unreasonable demands for special treatment, and a third in pressing upon the school educational ideas which conflict with those of the staff. It is of course the teacher's occupational hazard that the public, having been to

31

school itself, thinks not unreasonably that it knows about schools. But it is not surprising that the successful product of a well-reputed school should feel particularly strongly that he knows the answers. Such a parent may find it more difficult than others to realise that the accepted wisdom of twenty years ago is no longer current or at least not undisputed.

There can be no doubt that to open the door to parents produces its own problems. These would apparently not exist if the school adopted from a notorious primary school the notice-board: 'No parent beyond this point'. But that means only that they would not invade the headmaster's or House-master's study. Complaints and problems there must inevitably be and only a poor school would close its eyes and ears to them. Nor is the occasional tribute of thanks the only 'selfish' bonus which accrues to the teacher from this open contact. Almost equally welcome is the recognition by a parent that some course or objective previously opposed by him for his child does in fact seem to be suitable. The resulting sense of communion between parent and teacher must be of value to the child. And of course the teacher's advice is also affected in many cases by information which only the parent could give about the pupil's past experiences or predilections.

Not a few parents consult the teacher in despair over their children. Not simply, as might be expected, over academic failings, but over problems of personal relationships. It has comforted some to be told that the teacher has experienced in his own family precisely the same struggles and known the bitterness of almost total rejection by an adolescent son or daughter. Especially if he can add that peace did eventually break out, even if only after the offspring had become economically independent. And the schoolmaster, in his never-ending task of dealing with difficult children (when 'dealing with' implies the attempt at understanding and the building of bridges, not mere summary punishment), has much to learn from the parent, even if the latter does not realise what he is giving. It was a thought-provoking experience to have separate discussions with two couples about the unsatisfactory work and conduct of their sons, who were friends in the Fifth Form. Both boys acted irresponsibly and selfishly towards their parents, as they did

32

towards others. But one of them had parents of very limited means, including a father who could never work again. The other's parents were middle class, comfortably off and both well educated. There was a startling contrast between the former, who never failed in love, patience or generosity (going, as most people would judge, much too far in indulging their son) and the latter, who did not try to hide their dislike or contempt for theirs. The boys concerned are now young men. In neither case is the position good. But whereas the one is still in a happy relationship with his parents and at least on terms with society, the other has become an almost total outcast for whom no satisfactory future of any kind, nor even many years of life, can be foreseen.

The deduction emerges: did the latter parents care more about conventional standards of conduct than they did about their son? If so, were they mistaken rather than those others who thought differently? If they did not really prefer the convention to the child, did they try hard enough to make this clear? And what about us teachers who have traditionally claimed to stand *in loco parentis*? Which sort of parent is it that we seek to be towards our pupils?

Such close association with parents seems essential to the fulfilment of an educational ideal. What about a Parent-Teacher Association? That is a totally different thing. It may indeed be a desirable one but it can never take the place of the former nor, in an educational sense, can it achieve comparable good. A formal association of this sort is obviously valuable if it is seen as the only way of recognising and meeting with parents. It is much to be preferred to the absence of any contact. It may be a very useful means of raising funds and helping the work of the school. It may be a step towards democratic control of the institution, though it is doubtful whether that is intended as yet even by schools in which the PTA is particularly flourishing. One thing, however, seems almost certain: that such an association will tend to be led, and probably dominated, by articulate, middle-class parents.

In a school where the majority of parents are articulate and middle class (and some such do exist), this is natural and proper. But what of the rest? In most maintained schools the

33

middle class are in a minority. And it is the usual experience that, if these parents or even simply the educated, appear to 'take over' an association, those with lighter social and intellectual equipment tend to keep away. In this sense it is difficult to see how a PTA in a comprehensive school (given a normal spectrum of social background) could really be representative of the parents. That may not seem to everybody an objection. But it is at least arguable that an association of 'the teachers' and 'the parents' is not satisfactory if it is not truly representative.

In a rural area there are other practical difficulties. If the school draws half its children from within a radius of one mile and the rest from villages or hamlets anything up to eighteen miles away (which is the case at Wyndham), it is not easy to foresee representation which can be anything like evenly spread. And if, like ours, the school has no building which will seat more than about three hundred people, it seems idle to propose an association which cannot 'meet' in any more real sense than do the shareholders of a large company. The only practical association would appear to be by districts or villages: so far we have achieved only occasional meetings of this sort.

Accepting that an association of 'the parents' with 'the teachers' is not, in a corporate sense, a practical possibility with us, we eventually formed an association of 'The Friends of Wyndham'. This is still very young though it has begun in promising fashion. It is chiefly concerned with fund raising and with practical help in things like the annual Fair and the Jumble Sale. As such, it may not differ greatly from some PTAs. So long as it is recognised as an 'extra', a society of which the membership is voluntary, based on subscription and quite extraneous to the close association between teachers and parents for which we strive, the objections raised above do not seem serious. It is as yet too early to say how far this may be able to go in making known the views of its members and in affecting the direction of the school's policy.

So far as parents are concerned, 'democratic control of a school' (on the North American pattern) will be looked at askance by most English teachers. At Wyndham we have specific representation of parents on the Governing Body (besides the presence of four or five Governors who happen incidentally to have children in the school). Here again representation is something of a misnomer when it must occur by nomination, not by election, but it remains valuable. It ensures that the Governors are more fully (if not always accurately) informed through unofficial channels of what goes on in the school than it could possibly be claimed that they are through official reports. However, in a 'community school', through which the public circulates fairly freely at any time, where also both provision of meals and cleaning of premises are carried out by a force in which mothers of pupils make a very strong element, it may be doubted whether much that is visible can be kept secret from the outside world. For good or ill, the barriers are down between school and home. It is idle, and already too late, to regret the loss to exclusiveness. We rejoice instead at the gain to human contacts.

Many comments have been made by visitors on our habit, taken for granted within the school, of going to see the parent in the home. (In an area where telephones are relatively few, many of these visits have to be made, if the need is at all pressing or the teacher has only that evening available, unannounced.) It has been suggested that the visit might be resented by the parent or even by the child. This may simply reflect the view that 'school and home should be kept apart'. In practice, we have almost never encountered resentment. New habits grow up with a new school and the district seems to accept happily that we visit when we think there is need. A modicum of care is needed to avoid overlap between our visits and those of Welfare or other officers concerned with children. The counters to any difficulty are two: for us to remain in close contact with the officers of the social services (assisted by an occasional meeting over tea in school) and for the parent to see us in no official light but simply as friends of the child who think it advisable to discuss his problems from time to time.

Should the parent be seen in the classroom? This is so much more difficult to arrange in secondary than in junior schools that traditionally the former have confined themselves to set occasions like a Speech Day or, at best, to artificially staged lessons as part of a display of work. Perhaps the difficulty is simply the direct result of our being more old-fashioned in the secondary schools—of our holding on more firmly to the cell-like classroom, to the mystery of our teaching, to the implication that a lesson should be more of a penance than an enjoyable experience. At Wyndham we have not gone far yet: parents have indeed visited a considerable number of lessons but this has been by invitation of the teacher concerned. We have accepted that any spectators may be embarrassing to some teachers, that a large contingent is impossible to accommodate and that a probationer should not be visited. But though the practice grows slowly, it does grow. It is time that we too turned our attention to the classroom.

Chapter Six

Curriculum

What do they teach in those places? If the man in the street were asked this about infant schools or universities, he might be floored. But as regards secondary schools, his answer would be fairly confident. Of a dozen recognised subjects he would probably recall a number quite quickly. The curriculum he could retail may remind us of our grandmother's kitchen with its series of little tin boxes beautifully marshalled in rows, labelled and hermetically sealed from contact with each other or with the outer air. There are those of staple diet, like flour or mathematics, those (rather less essential) where a degree of choice operates—tea, coffee, languages—and those which may be seen as entirely optional like cloves, pepper, art or type-writing.

It is easy today to criticise this arrangement of fare in distinct compartments, though very difficult to alter it. Let us try a different image. The secondary curriculum is like the city of Troy. It is old. It is in a general sense well known, even if dilapidated. It is encrusted with myth and misunderstanding. But chiefly, like Troy, it turns out on examination to be not a single construction but a series of superimposed layers. Of nine cities on the site of Troy, probably each in turn was functionally devised. Later it became destroyed or unsuitable but often it remained to clutter the ground and hinder modernisation. The same edifice may in different ages fulfil different functions. It began as a house in which a man lived or the market-place where he made his living. Later it reappears as the temple where he worshipped with, possibly, more ceremonial than understanding. In just the same way the functional tail-coat of the hunting squire of the eighteenth century, passed on to his servant, became the indispensable adornment of the nineteenth-century butler.

This is rather like what happened to Latin. When this language was the *lingua franca* of the Church and of Europe, it was sensible to base education upon it. While it remained the common tongue of scholars, it was wise to teach it to all who were likely to go in for scholarship. But to teach it automatically to all our abler children today is absurd. Moreover, when voices are raised in defence of the classics, they are not usually pleading on behalf of the great and noble Greek literature nor even for that of the Romans, second-rate though it is. The cry is to stand by GCE 'O' level latin—a study pitifully limited in its scope and cultural value. To such irrelevancy has been reduced the staple diet of the mediaeval school, the very citadel, as it were, of Troy.

The other pillar of the ancient Grammar School curriculum, and at the time the less functional, was mathematics. Like the poor, it is always with us. Our reason for teaching it may vary from the cultural to the functional and back again at different times but the position is not to be assailed. Given that its nature had scarcely changed for a hundred and fifty years, it was high time that the fresh approach of 'modern mathematics' was introduced in the Sixties. Probably mathematics, as well as thousands of children, has had cause to be grateful to the innovators.

Science, of course, began to knock for admission already by the seventeenth century. Why then was it not until the twentieth that it gained a major place in the curriculum? It was largely ignored in schools of the nineteenth. We may recall the view held by Matthew Arnold. His understanding told him that science was very important. To give it a meagre ration of time in the school week was therefore foolish. To give it any more was not possible because of the entrenched position of the classics. On this reasoning he opposed its entry altogether.

When science was admitted, in the new secondary schools set up after 1902, it was essentially for the future clerk or technician, expected to leave school at sixteen or earlier. The education of a gentleman scarcely recognised it. Only since the second World War has the necessity for science been accepted, so whole-heartedly indeed as already, it seems, to provoke a reaction against it (though this may be because science, having

38

as yet only shallow roots in schools, is not well provided with the second generation of scholars, who should become the inspiring teachers of the third).

This long delay in the establishment of science teaching was a self-inflicted national disaster. It was probably more serious than would have been defeat in a major war—indeed, perhaps much more serious, since catastrophe in war often leads to educational advance.[1] But it was a natural legacy of our long spell as 'top nation'. The Pax Britannica was a fact of world history and it is not surprising if we were slow to change its basis. For our heyday coincided with the highest development of two ideals—nationalism and the Christian gentleman. We had had plenty of Christians in the Middle Ages and of gentlemen in the seventeenth and eighteenth centuries, but it was the rise of the middle classes on the tide of industrialisation which brought the two together. Added to this was the fear of the masses, almost pathological after 1793, and of intellectualism, which in 1848 was to appear almost equally dreadful. All these strands were combined in the education which was evolved for our most promising youth. It should honour Church and State. It should train leaders for both in acceptable ways of thinking. These should be free from the taints of internationalism, of trade and of speculation—which might lead to scepticism. If education looked back to the great days of Rome, it would provide a model both admirable and safe.

In those fifty years was set the glass of fashion and the mould of form. 'Set' is right. Able boys and girls between the Wars were still being educated along those lines and were still (surprisingly enough) accepting them on the whole without question. The dominance of the classics and of games, the subordination—if not the complete rejection—of art, craft, music and the spirit of inquiry, the concentration in both English and foreign languages on form and structure as opposed to expression, these are all well-known features. To this day the ultimate aim of our study in foreign languages (if we take that to be a university degree) is not active communication in the market-place but passive enjoyment in the study. (Although, ironically, in the Classical Tripos as we took it in the Thirties the time devoted to communication, through writing in prose

39

and verse with no possible living correspondents, far exceeded that given to study of the literature as such.)

Under this scheme of education science was kept, as we have seen, in lowly place and it was still regarded as creditable that a gentleman should profess no skill or interest in it. Fully excusable also in him was incompetence in modern languages. 'Classical' teaching presented us with only their skeleton. Our position as islanders and as the master race made it unnecessary to breathe life into the dry bones. These words were first drafted in a camp in Budapest. More pleasant even than the sun, the view or the fine equipment was the fact that virtually every nation in Europe was represented and that, with no central direction of any kind, between registering our presence and paying our bill, we lived in peace and communicated after a fashion. To join the Common Market may or may not be a Good Thing economically. As a venture in human relations it seems altogether attractive. For it to be successful as such, a new view must be taken in schools about what languages are for and about who is capable of learning them. Dutch, Scandinavian and Swiss are not more capable than English children in this respect. They are only better motivated.

Under the British Raj, so to speak, the aesthetic and practical subjects got short shrift. If the subject you taught did not entitle you to wear a gown, you did not look well on the prospectus or at Speech Day. If it lent itself to softness, it was suspect. If, like physical education, it could be confined to its tough and corporate expressions, this was desirable. Other subjects to suffer in our time of Empire were history and geography. In the Twenties we were still being taught essentially the capes, bays and products of the British Isles (and perhaps of our Empire), the dates and battle honours of our dynasties. These absurdly narrow bonds have, of course, long been broken. Even so, neither subject has perhaps yet caught up with the clock.

This may be unfair to geography, where the world view has come more easily. After all, if our great grandfathers were taught in school chiefly about places to which they might travel within a couple of days, the same formula may still produce a fairly appropriate answer today. With history, however, adjustment has been far more difficult. Forced to choose from an immense field of possible study, we are still not bold enough to say what is really important and what, in present perspective, has shrunk into relative insignificance. For example, neither of the French defeats, by Wellington at Waterloo (since Napoleon was already 'on the way out') and by the Prussians at Sedan, is now of first importance, but the latter has the greater relevance, even to us British, in 1973. Both of course are secondary in comparison with the invention of the steam engine which, among other things, made possible the triumph of Bismarck's army.

How trivial already seem those squabbles between what we choose to call nations. Indeed, how mistaken we were to see them in the light we have done, rather like athletic fixtures between schools or regions. Those militaristic histories were written in an age of nationalism, now largely discredited in the West. We at last reject the picture of 'The French' or 'The Greeks', wearing their appropriately coloured shirts, taking the field at the start of each season for another contest with 'The English' or 'The Persians'. We can see that far more valid were other motives: the desire for trade routes or natural resources, the ambitions of individuals or of groups, the clash between the interests of peasants and town-dwellers (sometimes appearing as a kind of class warfare), or the fear of ideas which seem likely, by discrediting former ways of thinking, to discredit also former systems of control. Such have been in turn Christianity, Protestantism, scientific automation, Marxism and multi-racialism.

But dissatisfaction with conventional history and geography is not enough. Suppose that within the next few years life is discovered on Mars or some other planet and contact established with dwellers there? To teach children about this new world and its inhabitants will be important. Shall we do this under the heading of history, geography, current affairs or some other subject? The question is trivial except as it may illustrate how our curriculum does not prepare for the world we live in. What are the main strands of thinking which fill the more intelligent Press and are conspicuously absent from the curriculum of nearly all who leave school at sixteen and of very many who do

41

not? We might suggest economics, sociology and perhaps psychology, politics and entertainment. It is tempting to add applied science, since it receives so little attention in many schools. And even though we have specified 'the more intelligent' Press, we ought still to add—sex.

If we were free to design the education of our adolescents as a preparation for being grown up, we might take a look at the incredibly confused and complicated world we have produced for them and search for clues to help them to understand it. Let us try a few questions.

Who are we who have at present the domination of this planet? By what steps have we come to our present state of development? How far are we still naked apes and how must we learn to control both ourselves and our fellows if we are to continue to survive? What about our fellow men—so different in economic circumstances yet identical in biological background? How can we overcome the barriers of language and of ideas in order to communicate with them? How does this economically and scientifically based civilization work? What are the forces which are latent in it for the destruction by us of ourselves or of our environment? How can we hold these in check? Assuming (as we must) that we succeed in this, what of the leisure which technological advance will press upon us? How can the school equip children to welcome and enjoy it?

What of the problems of mankind as a whole—how to feed man, how to control his reproduction and his lawlessness? How is he placed in space? Does anything exist beyond it? And can we sum up our universe in terms of space, time and energy or is there evidence of intangible, immaterial powers which may be of still greater account?

Faced with such questions, we can recognise that we are teaching in school much information that may be useful but very little understanding of the world which lies around as well as ahead of our pupils. Once more, it would appear, we are catering for those who have educated homes in which school subjects can be given relevance—and forgetting that most of our pupils do not have homes like that.

Many teachers in secondary schools have longed for a freer search for meaning and relevance. It has been granted to only a very few. Who are these privileged ones? Simply those who have the task of teaching children deemed unsuitable, because of their lack of ability, to undertake courses for public examination. The rest, the very large majority, must tread the well-worn path. It is true that the advent of CSE has given the chance of relative freedom to those who teach the middle band of ability. Only to a very small extent has it been accepted. The small proportion of papers taken under Mode Three (where the school devises its own syllabus) is evidence that freedom is not used.[2] As for our ablest pupils, it is their birthright to take more traditional examinations and to tread a well-worn path. Their syllabuses are devised by the universities.

It is true that there has been considerable change of late. Indeed, if it were only syllabus that was at issue, the outlook has so brightened that it could be called hopeful. But the requirement of passes in recognised subjects seems to rule out any attempt by the schools to tamper with the subject-based curriculum. And the movement of reform has been largely directed against premature specialisation. This is a proper, indeed a very necessary, object of attack. But the line taken has been to propose more examinations. We have seen major and minor subjects proposed for the Sixth Form, elective subjects, the 'I' level by the Headmasters' Association. We have been faced with the Qualifying and the Final examinations and even a date by which they were to have become operative. Mercifully, that has receded. But already we have both GCE and CSE to bedevil a comprehensive Fifth Form and sprawl across the entire summer term. And even if this welter of examinations is offered with an excellent objective in view, its effect must be to restrict even further the freedom of a school to plan a curriculum appropriate to the time. It is ironical to recall how we in England have acclaimed this supposed freedom and contrasted our happy state with that of most other civilised countries where (we believe) no such liberty obtains.

The fact is that it is only in the first three years of secondary education that we have even a modest freedom to choose what we shall teach. Probably only a minority of schools make good use even of this. At Wyndham we have sought to give freedom by holding no formal internal examinations until the end of the

Third Year and requiring no lists of marks or form orders. But we have made only slight progress towards any synthesis of subjects. History and religious education have been merged. We have a pilot scheme for including geography with these two. There seems no reason why english should not follow. But always two practical problems obtrude themselves. If the synthesis can be made, will there be forthcoming new teachers to undertake it when the present ones move? And, even if there were to be no changes in the team, how far would the claims of an immensely complicated time-table, in which every member has other commitments somehow or other to be reconciled with this one, allow the obviously desirable continuity of handling over a three-year spell? Both these problems are touched on later (see Chapters 14 and 15). But we must say here that the curriculum stands in need of a radical reappraisal which the schools are not able to effect.

Little has been said so far about practical subjects. Twenty years ago they played too large a part in the time-table of most non-selective schools, too small in that of the selective. The comprehensive movement has brought them into better perspective and they are no longer exercised in isolation. Art is linked with needlework, home economics with chemistry, metalwork with physics. The influence of project technology enlivens them all and what we see today is more akin to applied science than to the hobby subjects of the past. But, in the experience of Wyndham and some other comprehensive schools, there has been a surprising development (or rather, a lack of it) at the Sixth Form stage. Ten years ago we expected that longer staying in school and greater aspirations on the part of pupils once considered 'non-academic' would soon produce a large enrolment for 'A' level courses in the practical and aesthetic subjects. On the whole, this has not happened. Rather do the expected candidates turn to academic subjects. On consideration, the reason becomes apparent: society tends to regard secondary schools as sources of certification rather than of education. And the young must accept the values of their elders if they are to 'get on'.

This turns us back to the purpose of a school. In the debates of 1902 on the Education Act, scarcely a hint appears as to what the new secondary schools were for or were to attempt. One of the few clues came from A. J. Balfour himself. The country (he said) now had a system of elementary schools. It had, largely from private endowment, universities. What was needed was 'schools to bridge the gap'. The assumption that the secondary school is essentially a place of preparation for the university is natural but dangerous. Even in most selective schools only a minority of pupils will actually get there. If we gear our thinking too exclusively to these and to their needs, we shall give to the rest an education which lacks purpose, remains unfulfilled and is deficient in 'surrender value'.

The eye on the mountain peak is a good slogan for an aspiring climber. But the simile can be applied too readily to a school. The 'Everest expedition' or 'Apollo moonshot' principle works admirably towards the corporate, institutional aim of 'getting someone somewhere'. No doubt it worked well in ancient Egypt for those who held in their mind's eye the grand design of the Pyramids. But it must have appealed less to the Israelite slaves. We can hardly accept it for a school where every child is of importance. And it lends too much support to an unfortunate tradition of teaching in England, that we regard every part of the educational process as a preparation for the next one, a stage towards a goal rather than an experience satisfying in itself. Insofar as secondary education is seen as a process of certification, and the certificates are awarded by University Boards, a firm brake is applied to progress in developing the curriculum.

One must envy such a school as Summerhill. While it is not true that most independent schools have been innovators in the curriculum (for, to an extent possibly greater even than the maintained schools, they have been expected to provide their clients with what the latter want, namely certification), such a pioneer as A. S. Neill, operating on a tiny scale and with the support of parents who believed in him, could actually experiment. True, his experiments were more social and psychological than academic. But his liberty emphasises how far from free most schools are to develop a theory of education (in the sense of what to teach) and to carry it through.

NOTES

1 Prussia after Jena, Denmark after the loss of Schleswig-Holstein, are examples. In Britain we have not suffered general defeat for a very long time, perhaps too long for our good, but all our major Education Acts since 1870 have come at or near the end of wars —1902, 1918, 1944. After the fiasco of Suez it was only a year before we launched a 'new drive in secondary education'. The Americans acted similarly after the shock of the first Russian sputnik. It is the moral equivalent of arming the people when the enemy is at the gates.

2 At Wyndham Mode Three is used in about ninety per cent of all CSE entries.

Chapter Seven

Streaming

Streaming by ability has been well established in English education. But it does not have a long history. Clearly, it could not exist in schools which were not large enough to admit more than one class in each age-group. In the Harrow of John Verney ('The Hill') in the Nineties the system appears to have been one of vertical, rather than horizontal, grouping by ability. Boys found an initial place by examination and, as in the 'standards' of the elementary schools, might move upwards after only a term or remain stuck in the same form for even years on end. Between the World Wars both secondary and primary schools generally increased in size. In the Thirties there also came on the scene the concept of the Intelligence Quotient. Children could now be grouped as confidently according to their intelligence as they could by size or colour of hair. The two factors in combination produced streaming. In the Fifties it was almost universal in schools large enough to support it and was even found in the large Infant schools of urban areas. With its effect of a self-fulfilling prophecy, such a placing could amount to settling a child's academic future at '6 plus'.

One can recall hearing for the first time, in 1955, a group of H.M. Inspectors join in questioning the value of the system. This sounded radical but they were concerned only with grammar schools. Such schools, of course, operating within a system already streamed by selection and for the most part having a common curriculum, could well consider abandoning streaming. The more progressive began to do so in the Fifties. Only the most conservative still cling to it today. In many comprehensives the vastly more difficult problem of unstreaming is being eagerly tackled.

The strongest argument for rejecting streaming is that it creates the 'C (or D) stream mentality' for certain pupils, which is bad in itself, without the compensation of very obvious gain for the 'A', still less for the 'B', stream. It was in the early Sixties that the Head of a notable grammar school, after reading prayers to morning assembly, called out, 'Stand up the D stream!' All over the hall boys got to their feet. He proceeded to tell them in some detail that they were the scum of the school. The tirade led to the resignation of a young master but is not likely to have greatly improved the performance of the boys concerned. For it is the proclaimed view of their inferiority which chiefly handicaps children in low streams. In its purest form the system can be seen to be inhuman. It is almost certainly also unjust, in that it is impossible to place a large number of children, coming from different primary schools, in groups which are accurately differentiated by ability. The appearance of justice can be obtained by setting to all alike a common test, recording the results in precise form by means of marks, agreeing to disregard all other considerations and assuming that justice has thus been done. But no one familiar with the development of children can feel satisfied with such a process. It must be humbling to most of us today to have to admit that at one time we did not question it.

However, that is not the end of the matter. Merely to unstream *in toto* may not be the best possible approach. Indeed, the circumstances of schools (and even of subjects) differ so greatly that it is not to be expected that a single solution will fit all alike. To unstream either a grammar school or one in which neither extreme of ability is represented may be obviously sensible. The problem of a genuine comprehensive, housing both the brilliant and the seriously retarded (as is likely in a rural, if not in an urban, setting) is far more complex. And everything depends on the attitude, perhaps on the skill, of the teachers. For a Head to decree unstreaming while his staff is either unwilling or unable to tackle the resultant problems of teaching mixed ability groups has very little to be said for it. Let us examine in detail the problem of the school with a very wide range of ability.

It is important to realise that scientific proof of the efficacy either of streaming or of different systems is not really possible. This is because no group of children can be taught under both systems simultaneously and by the same teachers. To that extent a subjective element must always be present in the assessment, Next, we must face the fact that in the long run children of different ability will actually follow different paths. Some will go far in higher education, others will never reach the Ordinary level of GCE, even though increasingly they will tend to stay in school as long as their more gifted contemporaries. The aim should surely be to lead each child to the achievement of his full potential while not imposing on the slower developer the handicap of being classified inferior at an early, or ideally at any, stage. If it is he himself, rather than his teacher, who decides at some point that a particular course is beyond his powers, this is greatly preferable to his being excluded from it against his will. Much experience in schools today does, however, suggest that inability to reach a given objective or follow a particular course is often a case of 'not yet' rather than 'not ever'. Both pupils and their parents are far less likely to be discouraged if this is made clear to them.

There is obviously a point of principle at stake here. Do we accept that there is to be any differentiation of course within the school other than that introduced by voluntary leaving of some, mainly the weaker, pupils and voluntarily staying on to attempt further goals by others? The purist, or as some would call him the doctrinaire, may reject any such differentiation. At Wyndham we have indeed always refused to recognise specific sets in the Fourth Form as 'early leavers' on the grounds that to do so would be to endorse a decision taken, and perhaps taken unwisely, at too early a stage, namely near the end of the Third Year. However, it does seem that the effect on school work of public examinations to be taken in the Fifth should reasonably be recognised in the Fourth. Before the end of that year (and with a few courses even at the beginning of it) differing objectives in examination may have to be accepted. Given differing syllabuses and length of course (since CSE usually begins some six weeks earlier than GCE), it is desirable —though not always possible—to separate these groups of students. Some schools decline to do this. Some accept the right

49

of any student to opt for GCE rather than CSE, however slight his gifts. They are to be admired for their principles. It is to be hoped that the outcome of applying them is equally admirable. This is one of innumerable instances in which equally honest and idealistic teachers may choose different approaches. Incidentally, the dilemma would be far less acute if the obvious step of abolishing the dual system of examinations were taken, and some refinement (such as 'distinction questions' or a voluntary thesis) added to CSE led to the disappearance of 'O' level. Its demise is indeed now seriously under discussion, but its defenders are still strong.[2]

It is in the lower forms of the secondary school that there is a growing agreement on doing away with streaming. The initial placing can have such far-reaching effects that it should be as easily as possible revocable in the light of further evidence. Incidentally, in any new group of pupils as it enters the secondary school, there is one most important factor, sure to affect their development, which is very difficult to forecast: how will he or she adapt to the strange circumstances and the new teachers? Obviously, the child who has previously had, by reason of social circumstances, more opportunities to meet new people and to see strange places will have an advantage over his less fortunate fellow. We have found that some six months are needed by some children of narrow background and unvaried experiences to reach the state of confidence which others find within a week. Moreover, it is impossible to dogmatise on 'what should be done' because each school has, apart from a different staff, a different problem in placing its pupils.

The problem may well begin by considerable uncertainty as to their talents. If there are those who still regard the recorded IQ as being a reliable guide, even if of limited application, in this matter, they may be intrigued by the experience of Wyndham. After the 11 plus test was abolished, because all pupils were to come to the common secondary school, children in their last year at our twelve contributory primary schools continued to take a test of intelligence. Among these schools three different trends became clearly and disconcertingly apparent. In certain schools the range of IQ dropped perceptibly. On the whole this could be rationalised as indicating that the 'gain from coaching' was now absent. The children scored lower by five to ten points than their predecessors, apparently of similar ability, used to do but at least a cause could be ascribed and the order of attainment corresponded roughly to that of the teachers' assessment. In certain other schools the same high scores were recorded as in the past. Sometimes the result differed markedly from the teacher's opinion: an example was the child who recorded IQ 126 but was assessed as Grade C (on a five-point scale) with no apparent sense of incongruity, nor suggestion of under-achievement. It may not have been mere coincidence that these schools tended to be small, remote and staffed by elderly teachers. Finally, a third result of the abolition of the 11 plus—experienced in certain schools every year—was a completely irrational set of scores, the supposedly able often scoring IQ 90 or even lower, the dull registering usually low scores but sometimes over 100, the second or third test often registering lower than the first, and all correlation between score and teacher's assessment disappearing.

This highly confusing picture was largely clarified by the generally sound reports supplied by the primary schools, assessments which experience in the secondary school most often confirmed. However, any notion that there could on this evidence be set out an order of merit for the year-group was no longer tenable. If we had not already decided to abandon strict streaming, we should inevitably have found the virtue of doing so thrust upon us.

Before adducing our experience at Wyndham, we should consider a third alternative to complete streaming or unstreaming. This is the system of composing forms of fully mixed ability while 'setting' the children in all subjects. On the face of it, this seems sensible and just. In fact, something very like it occurs in our own and probably a majority of secondary schools once the 'Options stage' of the Fourth and Fifth Years has been reached. However, what may be appropriate for relatively mature pupils, familiar already with their school and their teachers, does not seem suitable for children of eleven. If they already have a considerable problem in adjusting to a

51

totally new environment, their chief need must be for security and stability. Only the most confident or capable could be expected to endure without harm a régime which regrouped them from hour to hour—and if the groupings were not in fact constantly changing, it would appear that we are back in the streamed situation.

If we reject this solution, there are two factors to be weighed against each other. One is the injustice of notional strict streaming—so brilliantly highlighted by our experience recounted above. The other is the capacity of teachers to deal satisfactorily with a wide range of ability, especially if their whole previous experience has accustomed them to teaching supposedly homogeneous groups.

The latter factor suggested to us that we should hasten slowly towards unstreaming. Our annual intake consisted of either eight or nine forms and, as we have said, both ends of the ability range were strongly represented. We began in 1964 timidly enough. Partly because no firm link of trust had yet been established with the contributory schools, we took the order of merit of the 11 plus test, operating for the last time that year, and deemed it perforce to be reliable. We contented ourselves with doubling all streams. Thus there were two parallel 'A' streams, two 'B', two 'C' and two 'D'. (For the way in which this original order was contradicted by later experience, despite its having been reinforced by a partially streamed situation, the reader may note the experience of that year group in Fifth Form examinations, as given in Chapter 3.)

By 1965 we were bolder. In principle we opted for two main groups of parallel forms—four 'A' and three 'C', with a single 'B' form as a cushion for the obvious invidiousness of a decision for a child between the two main groups, and a single 'D', or remedial, form. Experience was to show that the cushion form is not in practice a good idea because it is bound to be unduly disturbed by promotion and demotion. After this year we abandoned the classification of 'A', 'B', etc., as obviously not corresponding to any precise expectations. Later, we also abandoned the remedial form which had at first seemed a logical development. By 1967 we had established a norm of three 'bands' of ability: a top consisting of four parallel forms, a middle of two parallel and a lower of two more. As these last two forms were kept small, we had more than half the age-group in the top band, unstreamed within itself. It should be added that, as the system evolved, each year was left undisturbed in the organisation with which it started. After three years, of course, for each of them the system of 'Options', beginning in the Fourth, had the effect of abolishing the form structure and of introducing quite different groupings based on individual choice of subjects.

Then in 1968 it became clear that we should receive nine forms, not eight, in the new intake. After much discussion, we took the next step, of arranging only two bands, an upper of six parallel forms and a lower of three, parallel and smaller. Thus the ablest children we had were dispersed over six forms and the weakest over three. By now we had abolished the Remedial Department as such. However, with the only ESN provision in the county being residential and hence used only in extreme cases, two or three children in each year were found to be so retarded as to require special care in trained hands within the school. This makes of course a heavy demand on staffing but seems an essential step.

The year 1969 saw only eight forms of entry and we were able to continue the system of an upper band of six forms, this time with only two slower ones. But 1970 posed a new problem. There were again to be nine forms, but this time the reports on prospective entrants suggested that only two would consist of children needing special treatment. 'Seven plus two' happens to be a peculiarly difficult grouping to operate in our time-table, not so much in the First year as in the Second and Third when there are added problems of introducing a second foreign language for some but not all of the children. However, if the interests of the child were to come first, this was the one we must adopt.

There, at the moment of writing, Wyndham stood. It is forecast that the age-groups of the next few years will be a little larger—though forecasts even a mere twelve months ahead and based on actual numbers in the primary schools have proved remarkably fallible. If these forecasts do turn out correctly, the new factor may combine happily with another, that of slowly rising prosperity in the area and some consequent reduction in the educational problems that were caused rather by deprivation than by mental retardation. The next stage, of eight 'upper' and only one 'lower' form, may be near. When it comes, it will enable Wyndham to identify each of the eight with one of our Houses, a desirable end not yet fully achieved. Meantime, of course, we hope that staff become more skilled at handling forms of mixed ability. For that is the crux. Our responsibility is to develop the full potential of our children—both by avoiding discouragement in the placing and by flexible and challenging methods in teaching.

What has been the effect on the children of this progression towards mixed ability? In answering, the subjective element cannot be dismissed. Even if a total answer could be obtained by putting together the opinions of all teachers concerned (and a majority at Wyndham would certainly be in favour), it would include that of the idealist whose enthusiasm may blind him to his own failure to deal adequately with some of the problems arising in his class. It would include that of the sceptic, unwilling to credit that a system quite different from the one he had known in his previous career could be successful. It ought to take account of social factors: if a genuine attempt to select an 'A' stream on academic grounds had been made, ignoring the loss to others, how much harm—moral and even physical!— even to itself would have accrued from the fact that three-quarters of the form would have been drawn from Seascale? This is of course purely a local consideration. It may possibly not be exactly paralleled anywhere else, although the problem of the working class boy 'lifted' by his intelligence into the company of those more socially select and at home neither with his schoolmates nor with his neighbour in the evening is real enough.[1] The point of mentioning a local problem is precisely this: every school must have its own. To unstream is a social as well as an academic action. And while the philosophy of fair and equal treatment of every child must be basic to our thinking, few schools will be justified in brushing aside all practical considerations in pursuing it. Education, like politics, does on occasions become the art of the possible.

NOTES

1 This theme is further developed in Chapter 11, 'Social class and the common school'.

2 The 1972 proposals from the Schools Council for a common examination at 16+, unknown when this book was written, are very welcome.

Chapter Eight

Following progress in the large school

Unstreaming makes it, in theory at least, more difficult to follow progress. And the large school holds one permanent nightmare for its Head—that one day a parent will complain with justification of a state of neglect, whether in academic or other matters, which has been continuing for some time and has escaped attention. He (or she) cannot know everything himself. Delegation is essential. But it is his (or her) task to ensure that each child comes under informed care and that failings do not pass unnoticed. The work of sub-units is normally reliable but in academic matters it requires some reinforcement.

In the past, and usually in schools which were both smaller and more homogeneous in their composition than the comprehensive school of today, the answer was simple. Let there be marks. Let these be collected each month and the resulting form order published. Let an examination take place in all subjects towards the end of each term. Its results will be notified to the parent who can thus regard himself as very well informed.

This system does produce regular verdicts and constitute one method of tracing a pupil's progress. But the objections are weighty. First, the necessity to produce marks in some quantity (for a small collection would be liable to mislead) is stultifying to modern ideas of educating children. Second, the 'form order' (as anyone who has composed one knows only too well) is apt to give a misleading, in the sense of an arbitrary, result. It may well succeed in placing first the child who really is outstanding, possibly the first two or even three, but thereafter relative merit is assessed on very doubtful evidence. Is every subject to be given the same weighting? Is any notice to be taken of the fact that considerably more time is spent each week on one subject than another? Is religious education to be marked? Is art? Is physical education? If they are not, is this because they are more, or less, valuable educationally than those which do count in the total? If we say that in these subjects the marks cannot reflect the values envisaged by the teaching, is this not (or should it not be) also true of other subjects, imaginatively taught?

Some of these objections apply similarly to the regular internal examination. It can hardly be good for the teaching. So many values are aimed at in modern education which are extremely hard to test in the traditional way. In particular, we no longer see teaching as a process mainly of imparting information. We begin to recognise that examining is not educating: in any week given over to examinations no teaching is done. It is all too likely that none takes place in the following week either. At three times a year that would represent a loss of six weeks—virtually half a term [1]—to the teaching process.

But these objections are still relatively superficial. More essential is the fact that an efficient system of internal examinations and form orders does exactly what we have sought to avoid in moving away from streaming, that is to say that it encourages the few who scarcely need it and discourages the majority. True, children are adaptable and many learn to accept with philosophy that a prime function of their school is to demonstrate how much they are inferior to their fellows. But it cannot be good for them. Only the depressing argument that life is full of disappointments so that children are the better prepared for it by having plenty at school can be adduced on the other side. The trouble with us teachers is that we were mostly successful at school. We did not know the bitter taste of repeated failure. Those of us who have begun to learn it since are, alas! not always sufficiently disinclined to pass it on to our charges.

Let us start from a few assumptions. It is good for any child to be commended: he will work the better for it. Children (unless very young) are not apt to resent the praise given to their fellows, provided that it is generously impartial and avoids the odium of favouritism—which is indeed resented. It is, in general, depressing for a child (and he will work the worse

57

for it) if he is merely castigated. Nevertheless, he must not be allowed to work below his best (here, admittedly, is the most delicate of the assessments we are called upon to make). Finally, we must remain alert to what is his real state of progress. 'We' includes, of course, his parents.

There is probably no substitute at present for the report compiled by teachers at school and sent to the parents (who should be invited to add their comment). This is a pity, because the process of preparing the report is so exhausting. In a large school it may take two or even three weeks from first to last and involve a terrifying number of man-hours of labour. This is far more than its true value but we have not yet devised an improvement. The evenings set aside for discussion of work with parents (see Chapter 4, 'The child in the large school') are not a substitute because many parents do not attend and, if they all did, they could not possibly see all the teachers concerned. Moreover, these discussions are all the more useful, and actually kept shorter, if the parent has already read a recent report on his child's work. Finally, the report is (or should be) the best cumulative school record.

At Wyndham we have shaken our heads many times over the enormous labour, in comparison with the results achieved, involved by the school report (as an example, it claims from the headmaster and some others several times during the year a complete weekend given over to nothing else). In course of time we have devised certain palliatives.

(i) We have reduced the norm from three reports to two, although the report form is planned for three entries each year and we designate a minority (between ten and twenty per cent) of pupils to be given a report in those terms when their companions do not have one. If, for example, the form has a report at Christmas but not at Easter, we may expect that an Easter report will be called for (by the Head of House) on four or five members whose progress is causing concern.

(ii) We have staggered the times of issue so that proper attention may be given to the 'year' which is currently having its report. Some times are more valuable than others. For example, there can hardly be any point in issuing a report on a Fifth Former late in the summer term. The last occasion when it seems worth while to report to their parents on the work of these pupils with a genuine hope that improvement may be brought about is the previous February, together with the results of trial examinations. (The suggestion that a summer report is needed for prospective employers we reject. They always receive a special report on each pupil who applies to them.)

(iii) We have reduced the physical labour for teachers (while increasing it for clerical staff) by making the report into a folder of detachable subject sheets. Much time goes into sorting and re-sorting the sheets but the person whose skilled labour is most in demand, the teacher, no longer endures the frustrating queue in the Common Room to 'get at the document'. He takes home quietly the sheets concerning the pupils he teaches —in which no other colleague has at that moment any interest. As the sheet is designed to cover all the terms for the first three years (a different sheet covers Fourth and Fifth stages, while the Sixth Form are dealt with again differently), the system makes it impossible for the teacher to avoid seeing what he (or a colleague) wrote last time. Thus tedious repetition or failure to notice a very marked change in the child are both made unlikely. Finally, since all reports are written in isolation from other teachers, the echo effect, when those who do not hold strong views hesitate to differ from their colleagues who have already commented, is avoided. If (which is rare) identical opinions are given, the verdict is all the more impressive because of the circumstances.[2]

By these means we hope that some of the most depressing features of report-writing have been reduced or avoided. There is therefore the better chance for teachers to see the report as a constructive step in the relationship between them, the child and the parent. Nothing is gained by disguising the truth but much can be lost by speaking it harshly. The cutting or sarcastic remark has no place in a school report. There are, of course, comments which indict the teacher rather than the pupil. 'He has handed in no homework for weeks' (why have we not learned of this sooner?); 'she spends her time chattering to her friend' (why were they not separated?); or 'I can do nothing with him/her'—all these, if they represent the first communication on the subject, are confessions of failure. The best comment is the one which impresses the reader as being obviously 'about this child and no other.'

In earlier years, although we did not include marks (except from formal examinations, which are not held until late in the Third Year) we gave a grade, on a five-point scale, to every child in each subject. This was for attainment in relation to his form. It could not be calibrated to the whole age-group, because this would mean in a comprehensive school that some children never had any grade in any subject above E and others, without even necessarily working hard, never any below A. However, as we have moved further and further towards the completely mixed ability group, the grade has clearly become less helpful—for the reasons set out above. This becomes obvious to a headmaster when he realises: 'By my own action, before this child was even personally known to me, I have settled whether he shall have a good set of grades in a "middle bracket" form or a poor set in a form which includes some of the ablest of his year. Yet he is the same child and, probably, working about equally well in either case.' His next thought must surely be: 'We must revise the system.'

Our solution at Wyndham has been to continue to award grades twice a term for the first three years, as in the past, but to keep the knowledge of them confidential to the staff. This avoids the depressing effect on the child of being given a series of low grades which he has not deserved through any failure to do his best. Yet the Head of House, who summarises the report as might be done elsewhere by a form teacher, is able to give the true picture in words. Thus the parent is not deceived nor the child unreasonably depressed. Of course, if low grades have been earned by idleness, there is probably a good case for informing the pupil!

From the Fourth Form onwards, the issue of grading relative to other pupils becomes unimportant. What matters is the child's progress in relation to the course and the objective he has undertaken. And as the objective becomes even more vital to the child's future, so greater precautions must be taken against a lapse in application. We have a system of internal assessments given at the end of any month in which neither a

60

report to parents nor an official examination has occurred. This 'taking of the temperature' enables a Head of House to alert parents by letter or in person to a worsening situation.

In the Sixth Form we have just decided to go further. We have supplemented (and may well supersede) the periodic report by a continuous 'fever chart', so to speak. This is maintained in the Sixth Form office and will, it is hoped, from time to time be sent home for the weekend so that the parent will get the earliest possible warning of a downward turn of the graph.

This chapter has dealt with technical matters, perhaps of little interest to the general reader. To the teacher they are important. To the public they need carry only a general message—that there is no need for the large school to be thought of as an insensitive organisation.

NOTES

1 There is yet another objection, which strikes at the root of the professed aim—of keeping the parent informed. All figures are relative. On the mere tally it is impossible to say whether a given score is a good one (on a stiff paper) or poor (on an easier one), whether this child, who has indeed beaten his neighbour, is to be congratulated on doing so when all strove hard or is the only one to have achieved a satisfactory performance. The point is emphasised by the report form used and passed on by many Scottish primary schools. No doubt other heads of schools have puzzled many times over what this impressive collection of marks and grades actually signifies. It may be that in Scotland the meaning is clear. South of the Border, however, one would gladly give it all in exchange for even such a simple remark as 'he is of average ability', 'she is very keen on reading but poor at arithmetic' or 'his talents are rather limited but he always works to the best of them'.

2 It must be recognised that this system is probably too subject-orientated for contemporary taste. Nevertheless, it does (unfortunately) fit the facts of the present teaching situation. In our Reception House (for first year children) the staff have adapted the system to take account of the fact that, wherever possible, several subjects are in the hands of a single teacher.

61

Chapter Nine

Sixth Form

The Sixth Form is a peculiarly English phenomenon. We think of it as the pride, the apex and the justification of a secondary school. It has been held to be the reason why we must not have comprehensive schools (because if we did, the schools could not support a viable Sixth Form without becoming larger than we like). It has been seen as the arena for which lower forms are a preparation so that we cannot analyse the school, or more particularly the curriculum, as a whole without seeing that it is conditioned by the Sixth Form. For that reason we shall give in this chapter some attention also to lower forms.

There is an English semantic difficulty in discussing the Sixth. It is not a form in the sense that others are or used to be. In a grammar school it does not represent the Sixth Year but usually the sixth, the seventh, part of the eighth and (not infrequently) some of the fifth. Moreover, in the public schools where it originated (and they are not, of course, public but private), the only way in which this odd form can be designated Sixth is by suppressing the earliest numbers and starting with Third or Fourth. Yet the less precise the concept, the more sacred the cow. We are prepared to die in the last ditch for, or even with, it. To continue the metaphor, the Sixties have seen a further muddying of the waters in the ditch of the Sixth Form as new currents have flowed into it. But first a glance back to an earlier period.

It is worth reminding ourselves how small, until very recently, was this sacred cow. We speak, of course, not of independent schools where it was normal to complete the course by staying until eighteen, whether or not this brought academic achievement, but of maintained grammar schools. The original vintage, of 1902, was essentially an 11–16 school and indeed fortunate if it kept the bulk of its pupils throughout that span. To it the tiny excrescence of a Sixth Form was added where possible. (This did not mean that, to change our metaphor, the tail was not allowed to wag the dog.)[1] Even in the Fifties, when an average grammar school might have a roll of three hundred, H.M. Inspectors wrote of 'the main school' as opposed to the Sixth Form. By the criterion then considered suitable, the latter 'should' (perhaps a quaint auxiliary) include ten per cent of the total. This meant that in those days we had in England in school on their seventeenth birthday probably seven per cent, or fewer, of the age-group. It was the discovery in Vancouver in 1956, with a voluntary school leaving age like ours of fifteen, that the corresponding statistic there was eighty-five per cent which first brought the writer to think that there might be something after all in not revealing to children at age eleven that their academic future was limited.

The main school was a place of general education, at least as that term was understood. The Sixth Form was the place for specialisation or, in the vernacular, 'study in depth'. Both these phrases deserve to be analysed. Education which is general must surely include a balance of arts and science subjects, some element of the practical and the aesthetic, and no such slanting in any direction as to ensure, through omission of important elements, that no other course can be followed at the next (Sixth Form) stage than the one already being pursued.[2] At Wyndham this is achieved in the Fourth and Fifth Forms to this extent, that no course offered in the Sixth Form is debarred to any pupil in the Fifth *except one in a language which he is not already studying*. In the violent discussions which have raged round this subject in recent years many schools have rejected the charge against them of premature specialisation. The term is obviously a subjective one, like illiteracy ('he is illiterate who is less literate than someone else thinks that he ought to be'). But it is to be feared that the example of boarding schools, where art, handicraft and drama can be pursued out of class hours yet strictly within the curriculum, has been adduced too readily to day schools operating under different conditions.

'Study in depth' is an even greater shibboleth. It means:

study of very few subjects. As our university tradition has abhorred general degrees in favour of close specialisation, and we have seen our Sixth Formers as quasi-undergraduates in their studies (though not in their personal freedom), so we have cherished the narrow concentration which brings to an end their general education. To a boy (this is rare in girls' or mixed schools) who is sufficiently able, this can happen at the age of fourteen. The plan is not followed outside this country. Looked at dispassionately, it seems ill-advised. Its best defence is probably that it is designed, like so many of our general plans, for the quite unusually able pupil. He (or she) is indeed exceptional. We may allow that his case merits special treatment—though not that the same treatment should apply to the many others less gifted in our Sixth Forms. It is therefore appropriate to call, as witness *against* study in depth, Mr W. R. Elliott, Senior Chief Inspector of the Department of Education and Science. Himself an outstanding scholar, he has a son no less distinguished in ability. In thirty years of the Inspectorate, Mr Elliott has had probably unique opportunities for observing the practice and the effects of study in depth. Here is the view he gave to the Headmasters' Association, an audience not naturally sympathetic to it, when speaking on 'Further Education and the Sixth Form'.[2]

This brings me to the *curriculum*, on which we could spend a long time. But it is not for me to tell you much about this. We must of course consider both the range of study desirable today and also the degree of choice for our pupils to make. We must also remember the logistics. Feelings can run high on these issues as well as on others, and I must declare my position. May Crowther rest in peace. I am for the wider range of study and I note with interest and sympathy what you say in your booklet on *The Sixth Form of the Future*. I am too good a European to align myself with the English diehards. The breadth of vision which is said to emerge from study of a couple of subjects in depth has always seemed to me a matter of grace rather than natural consequence. To me the new Sixth Form is a providential event, and I do not grudge any of the torment it may cause us in reassessing the curriculum or our examination techniques.

Such a witness must be heard with respect. We shall not do more with regard to the great debate about Sixth Form curriculum than to assert that the English should not be seen as the only ones in step. No plan so far put forward meets the need to maintain a wider field of study for all, or most, Sixth Formers while catering also for the less able who now join them in such numbers. No plan has yet carried the merit of reducing the excessive number of examinations taken by our pupils between fifteen and eighteen. But some plan is required. We cannot continue to live in the world of the Fifties, to which this chapter now briefly returns.

Between Main School and Sixth Form there was, before 1951, a great gulf fixed. It was called the School Certificate. It served to keep the Sixth Form select. Indeed, it might even be looked on as the sole justification of the narrow curriculum followed by a Sixth Former that a relatively balanced certificate had first been obtained. The introduction of GCE technically abolished the gulf. This step, however, proved generally unpopular in the schools affected by it and they were free (except, for a time, in the matter of the famous age bar) to take what action they thought fit. (We may pause to consider what that sentence implies. It is this: a great many Heads were free every year to tell still more children, without appeal, that their full-time education was finished. Many did so.) In practice, most schools kept much the same barrier, in the sense of a specified qualification for entry to the Sixth Form, as before. After all, if the process of education is seen as refinement of a mass through winnowing down, it is essential that the mass should be diminished. However, in course of time, things began to change.

First, for whatever reason, children began to stay longer in school.[3] Then, for whatever reason, a new Burnham pay award began to categorise schools according to their size, giving weight to the presence of older pupils through a pointage system. Following, whether or not consciously, the example of North America, a rush for higher education began to build up.

Despite an enormous increase in the number of places available there, the new large Sixth Forms began to be dominated by competition for them. UCCA was born. Here were the ingredients of a quite new sort of Sixth Form.

If the Sixth Form had two hundred, three hundred or even four hundred members, an immediate consequence was that only a small minority could be prefects, games captains, even members of first Fifteens. But surely this was what they were there for? Probably not even Mr Chips would have put the question quite so bluntly, but we may fairly admit that something like this was in our minds before the War and some of it survived even twenty years ago.

If intensely competitive study was now necessary in order to breach the walls of higher education, so that all members were now in the position of the one-time 'swot' who aimed at an Open Scholarship, was it right for schools to fill up the time of Sixth Formers by requiring of them a host of administrative duties? These might be petty, amounting almost to 'baby sitting' (a reflection of the principle: 'Children are not to be trusted') or graver than general opinion can now approve, like caning other pupils, but in either case they took up time.

Again, increasing affluence (in itself a serious obstacle to study) was bringing more opportunities for the use of leisure, whether or not creatively, and ever greater sophistication. With better health, puberty arrived earlier. Before the decade ended, Sixth Formers were to become voters. Even earlier, some would have borne children and, contrary to tradition, not been expelled from school. It became increasingly obvious, a point we have made earlier, that all pupils are not children and that differential treatment is needed. Schools, we have argued before, should not be dominated by restrictions. But if they do have many rules, unless means can be found of exempting senior pupils from them, the latter will feel them most, which seems inappropriate. Moreover, if the seniors are to act as enforcers of the rules (their traditional rôle), then any breach, as in a minor matter like smoking,[4] becomes more serious in them than it would be in a younger child: while he has merely broken a rule, they have betrayed a trust. Yet it is we, 'the management', who have in a sense created the offence by enacting a

66

restriction for young children, applying it to adolescents and then insisting that those to whom it is least appropriate should set the example in observing it. The alternative, not unknown, whereby the prefects break all the rules but pretend not to do so and are allowed to get away with it, seems highly unsatisfactory in a school, though it is a position time-honoured in some prisons.

All these developments were present and the writing on the wall to be seen in any grammar school in the Sixties. But the movement towards the comprehensive school added a further complication. Were we to have comprehensive 'Main Schools' and selective Sixth Forms? If we did not accept this, and it seemed anomalous, what were we to make of the new Sixth Formers for whom the previous barrier on entry would have to be set aside? What courses could we offer them? And while we strove to make the régime of our Sixth Form more liberal to suit the greater maturity of its members, was not the attempt bedevilled by the arrival in some strength of others who were, intellectually at least, less mature than those we were used to admit?

Thoughts such as these had been worrying the writer, as Head of a school with a mainly conventional Sixth Form, when he found himself appointed to Egremont in 1963. The school to be opened the following year included in its plan a 'semi-independent Sixth Form College'. It is true that there was, wisely, no brief concerning the existence of prefects, uniform or other details, but the intention was clear that the Sixth Form should be separate from the Houses which made up the rest of the school (see Chapter 4). This decision caused more concern to parents and visitors than perhaps any other of the many departures from convention we have offered them. So deeply ingrained is the sense that a secondary school's principal function is to teach 'leadership' and the only aspect of this idea to which we have been accustomed is that of being a prefect. This selective school view was so strong that it prevented contemplation of the same subject through the eyes of children who were less able and would in fact never reach the Sixth Form. Yet these, for many years to come, would constitute the majority. (At the time of writing, about forty per cent of our comprehensive intake stays to enter the Sixth Form—that is, considerably more than would have been admitted to a selective school but still less than half the age-group. If leadership was so important, and was to be exercised by the Sixth Form, these others would all be denied it. If, however, the Houses, small as they were, contained no pupils above the Fifth, there would be opportunities of 'taking responsibility' given also to those who would finally leave school at that stage.

In the event, one practical question was settled for us. Since we had no Fifth Form on opening, we did not accept transfers into the Sixth. The following year, 1965, saw the Sixth Form opened, but it consisted necessarily of members new to the school and with no roots in the Houses. Their independence was thus assured. The seal was set on it by their not being required, or rather being required not, to wear uniform. This produced some reaction: the girls, conservative creatures, decided that they wanted a uniform of their own. Although we were sorry about this (and numbers were too small to warrant a special design), it was decided to choose a line from a well-known retailer and a special journey was made to Carlisle for the purpose. Selection proved almost as difficult as the judgement of Paris but was fraught with less awkward or lasting consequences. For within three weeks, with only a minority equipped, the line ran out. Nothing has been heard of uniform since.

We began with only twenty-five students. By 1970 the number has reached one hundred and sixty-five and should go on rising steadily. The raising of the school leaving age will probably give the movement to stay longer a further stimulus. If present trends continue, it seems likely that expansion, though slowing down, will never stop. The original small entry was almost a selective one, since the unqualified Fifth Former is not likely to apply to a new Sixth Form College, at least until there are plenty of others like him known to be doing so. Now, however, a routine has been established and we can begin to see a pattern of needs and problems emerging.

First is the need (and the problem) to give independence and yet foster responsibility. There are no written rules in our Sixth Form College, though this does not distinguish it from the rest of the school. From the beginning it has attempted self-government through a committee, normally meeting without the presence of any staff, and the success of this method has varied. Increasing numbers have tended to weaken it but they have also given a wider choice of good committee members. Experience has taught the students more discretion in deciding who is suitable to be elected. We stand on the brink (we hope) of seeing the Sixth Form Committee take a lead in a Council of the whole school.

Meantime responsibility is being seen in a new context. Formerly, as we have noted, it meant 'taking responsibility' and this was defined as exercising over others a delegated authority. That suited well enough the needs of a more authoritarian age. We should now put the word in a different setting. 'Acting responsibly' seems more appropriate to a citizen of today. And that is a virtue which everybody has the opportunity to exercise—provided only that he is not bound hand and foot by regulations. It is true that from time to time there is a specific responsibility for him to take (for example, being willing to serve on a committee or to volunteer help to a community project) but this is not the norm. Nor would 'acting responsibly' in this sense appear to be dependent on, or even obviously fostered by, service as a prefect in the traditional way.

'Responsibility with independence' is of course most called for in the student's own work. If we spoon-feed him, he will be prepared neither for higher education nor for responsibility. He certainly needs to be given the opportunity to waste his time (which will be so freely his in most universities) and yet, because he is still adolescent, we have to keep check on the extent to which he is doing this (see Chapter 8, 'Following progress'). As regards responsibility towards others, it has seemed to us part of a proper training that everybody should give service on occasions (rather than selected people all the time). Some of this may be to the community outside the school. Particular occasions like the school's Summer Fair or the annual Jumble Sale for charity call for a contribution from seniors as from others. There is work to be done in organising the library or out of school activities, refereeing games and so

69

on. The development from 1969 of our Reception House for First Year children has given a special occasion to seniors of both sexes (particularly those who plan later on to teach) to take part and they have responded well. Particular instances are: they sit with and supervise children at meals, organise games or other activities and guide the young child's instinctive response to appeals for charity. With these children the Sixth Formers exercise an authority which is not resented, as it may tend to be in senior Houses where the next, unprivileged age-group is so very little younger.

Of course the greatest problem in a comprehensive Sixth Form is that of providing suitable courses. About half of our Lower Sixth presents no problem because it follows conventional Advanced level courses plus General Studies. Another quarter is not difficult to cater for because, with no pretensions beyond Ordinary level, it follows an essentially Fifth Form type of programme. The remaining quarter is the difficult one. These students have had enough success in the Fifth Form not to be able to find their course at that level but too little to attempt more than possibly one 'A' level subject. We have commercial and business studies courses which suit some. These include some 'O' level options not available lower down the school, such as Accounts and Commerce. We have added others like Human Biology, Sociology and British Constitution so that courses are available for pupils to take and gain additional qualifications. More should become possible as numbers rise. We have discussed joining forces with the nearest College of Further Education (unfortunately not very near) and have seriously considered the merits of part-time attendance at school. It may be an indictment of our system to say that, outside the General Studies options, courses are assumed to be for examination. But the difficulty of finding employment in West Cumberland (the district at the moment of writing has seven per cent unemployed) is such that it would not be kind to the student to allow him to embark on a course without the prospect of improving his chances on the labour market.

General Studies has to be woven into the pattern. It is always there for the conventional 'A' level student, with a partial reservation for those who need to take up Latin in the Sixth

Form. Physical education is optional but the student is called upon to show that he is employing his time positively if he does not take it. Other courses are normally of a term's duration with a guided (or at least supervised) choice among them to see that over the two years some balance is obtained between the subjects taken. We have been keen that everybody should undertake at least one practical subject, at least one academic and at least one term on current affairs. All students have a weekly tutorial group hour which gives the opportunity to survey their programme.

One promising development in General Studies was abandoned with regret. This was the opportunity offered by the Cambridge Syndicate to choose our own 'A' level subject (or pair of subjects) and examine the students ourselves, partly through course work. 'Russian Studies' (combining Literature, History, Geography, Economics and Music) together with Twentieth Century Science, which we selected, made an attractive course and the experiment was in itself successful. Unfortunately, over the two years in which we taught it, our Sixth Form was becoming genuinely comprehensive, as it had not been in 1965. Sadly, we came to the conclusion that in a community containing many students capable of 'A' level and many others, a General Studies course examined at that level could only be divisive, the reverse of what we intended. For this reason we did not repeat it.

Five years is a short period, though perhaps less so when we speak of a community in which most students spend only two. It is to be hoped that it is not complacency which makes us feel that the original concept was right and its implementation mainly successful. At least we feel more inclined to extend its freedom to younger pupils than to reimpose the restrictions of the past on our Sixth Form. It may be of interest that, as forecast in December 1970, some fifty-five per cent of the entire original age-group expect to stay into the Sixth next September.

NOTES

1   For the emphasis, however inappropriate, on preparation for university, see the last part of Chapter 6, 'Curriculum'.

2   Address given to the annual General Meeting of the H M A at Canterbury on 10th April 1969. Mr Elliott retired as S.C.I. in 1972.

3   In order to date this phenomenon, we may recall that in 1954 the Central Advisory Council's report, *Early Leaving*, painted a very gloomy picture indeed of the reluctance of children, even in Grammar Schools, to complete the Fifth year.

4   Even the serious medical consequences now found likely to arise from smoking do not alter two facts which make it inappropriate to describe smoking as a major offence: that many parents and teachers smoke without incurring censure; and that if we do inveigh against it probably more pupils will smoke than would otherwise have done.

Chapter Ten

'Discipline'

This is a word honoured in English education. The head of any school is likely to be asked by visitors: 'What do you do about discipline?' Very often the term is a euphemism for punishment. The concepts are of course different but both are to be considered in this chapter.

An article [1] about the Headmaster of Eton described some of his many responsibilities and the routine of his day. We learned that 'daily at 12.15 he metes out justice' and ex-soldiers might recognise the traditional 'CO's orders'. Some offenders are caned. This was not in itself surprising, though it would be so in many countries. What really amazed was that a task of this sort should form part of the duty of England's leading headmaster—with 1,200 boys in his care.

A school, however small, is likely to be made up of enough people to require some control to be imposed on movement (though it is interesting to speculate how many people are to be found at, say, Charing Cross at 5 pm on any weekday moving fast and controlled by no more than the clock, common sense, some more or less agreed conventions and a modicum of consideration for others). If some minimal control is thus called for, it is remarkable how much more has been traditional in English schools. They are, of course, ultimately monastic in origin but so are those of many other countries. We have Puritans among our ancestors. But so do many French, Dutch, German and Scandinavian teachers. Why is it that we practise, and pride ourselves on practising, a more restrictive 'discipline'? What are the implications of this word?

That the flesh should be mortified—the idea comes from the monastery: that children (and adults too, for that matter) should be prevented from doing anything which they enjoy—

here speak the Puritans: that personal idiosyncrasies are undesirable, and that in a community everyone should behave and dress in the same way—that is the view of the institution, more particularly of the regiment. Again and again we find ourselves following in English schools ideas evolved in boarding schools and worked out in the barracks of the Guards. That is why we differ from the Continent. It is worth remembering that in the nineteenth century the European world as a whole wore uniform—that is, clothes indicative of the class or occupation of the wearer. The conventional aristocrat differed from the working man only in that he was allowed and could afford some variations (though not in the evening) and that he was expected to change his costume several times a day.

To this background we owe our regimental concepts: that the pupil, like the soldier, must be dressed distinctively from other people, but exactly like all his fellows, in a costume of the past, complete with headgear; that his movements as well as his conduct should be controlled as much as possible; and that one of his most important functions is to show outward respect to those placed in authority over him. The cap is an aid to saluting.

'The good school,' writes Sir Alec Clegg, 'does not make children behave well. It makes them want to behave well.' This is a profound saying, though not an easy one. When you come to think of it, if it were sufficient to 'make children behave well', the methods of a prison should commend themselves to a school. Restrict liberty and supervise movement as much as possible. Then nothing can be amiss. But Sir Alec's point is that unless there is opportunity for things to go awry, they cannot truly go well. Good 'discipline' cannot begin until close supervision is withdrawn.

If we accept this proposition, discipline must be seen in a different light. The more we try to make people (and this includes children) do things, the less likely they are to do them willingly. Admittedly, guidance will probably be needed where conformity to some convention is needed for practical reasons, e.g., that circulation in restricted spaces is easier if we observe a 'rule of the road'. Again, we are all forgetful, especially young children, and we shall probably need reminding before we can

74

learn such a useful habit. But good discipline postulates that obedience to an idea or a request comes from within, from a recognition that the idea is reasonable. The aim is a relaxed atmosphere where we decide for ourselves that this is a suitable, and a considerate, way in which to behave.

This sort of discipline does not catch the eye and may be suspect to those who hold a more traditional view. At Wyndham we have heard the complaint that 'the children do not respect the staff'. If the teachers concerned are clearly worthy of respect by any criterion, the sentence would seem to reflect on the pupil rather than on them. It probably means that he does not fear them.

Should he? This does not seem desirable. The contrary, that no one should feel afraid in school, is surely to be hoped. Unquestionably, it will produce some problems. The effervescent pupil will make more disturbance, the ill-disposed be more surly, at least on some occasions, than they would if they had reason to fear anger or pain. But in the long term, only in an atmosphere of freedom from fear can the best discipline be expected.

'Anger or pain.' We shall deal with the latter when we come to speak of punishment. Let us first consider anger. Here are two propositions. First, that restrictions irk and provoke disobedience—that, for example, there would be less smoking if it were not forbidden. Second, that anger is at all times a bad counsellor. We recognise this in dealings with adults. But the Old Testament concept of 'righteous anger' was still honoured at the time when many school traditions were formed. In adult life we no longer 'cut' in public someone deemed guilty of moral failure. In this respect we are more charitable than our grandparents. But schools reflect the past. And it has been common, almost expected, among teachers in secondary schools to speak with anger both to and concerning child offenders. Few, if any, of us avoid this pitfall. But it is always a weakness.

In staff meetings we lose sense of proportion if we inveigh against children collectively, more particularly because we cannot claim to be faultless ourselves. The faults of which we complain are usually those of carelessness or forgetfulness. Yet hardly ever did the excellent staffs which can be instanced here normally succeed in carrying out exactly and on time the requests made periodically to them as a body. This should temper our emotion both when we discuss children and when we correct their faults. The vision of a headmaster as Olympian, often angry, comes down to us from an earlier age and hinders our work. There is a line difficult to draw, but very well worth drawing, between making light of a child's error and making too much of it. The latter course is likely to do the greater harm.

Not all offences are equally bad. (It might be fair to add that very few are as bad as we tend at first to think.) And not all offences are equally bad when committed by different children. That would seem self-evident. But the whole concept of 'school rules' denies it. This is a very good reason for having no written rules in school.

What is a rule? It is surely more than a convention or a practice (such as walking on the left to ease traffic). Presumably it implies some retributive action on the part of authority if it is not observed. It must also be enforceable. Attendance at school is a rule, though made by a higher authority, and enforceable, up to a point, though again not directly by the school. The wearing of uniform is a practice. In the last resort it cannot be enforced, even if that were desirable. Could we define a rule as a demand made by the school, the breaking of which must, if persisted in, lead to exclusion from the community? There do exist actions on which exclusion might be based. Unrestrainable cruelty or even incorrigible insolence and disobedience are of this sort. But, it would seem, these are not things about which we make rules. 'No child shall be persistently cruel or incorrigibly rude . . .'? If the definition of a rule suggested above were accepted, it would seem that we never make rules about important things, only about the relatively trivial. Those on which a good community might be based—'Thou shalt be considerate towards everybody'—are unsuitable as rules because they will be broken by everyone at times and by some very often. A simple solution (followed at Wyndham) is to have none. It seems to produce no catastrophic—nor even a perceptibly bad—result.

In place of school rules, in order to guide the thinking of a diverse and rapidly growing community, we wrote a 'Code of Conduct', which goes to all new staff. It defines what we are aiming at in atmosphere and convention and it urges them to seek the same ends. It avoids saying at any point: 'All children must do this or not do that'. This did not satisfy everybody. The belief that good discipline in a school is achieved by a set of precise rules backed up by the use of force (rather than by a united effort of example, vigilance and, if necessary, admonition) dies hard in the profession. However, when in response to request we tried to codify these rules, they proved neither few nor simple. The attempt was sincerely made but did not appear to alter the situation.

And now, to punishment. It is perhaps one of our least successful activities in schools. Suppose we had none? It is not likely that the offender would be much affected. Punishment is scarcely ever redemptive although withholding it sometimes is. It is for the benefit of the others—*pour encourager les autres*— that we punish. Does it encourage, that is to say, deter? This is doubtful. The fallacy about deterrents is that the offender counts on not being caught—if he counts at all.

Corporal punishment is an old institution in England. It accords with both the mediaeval traditions and those of the last century—the philosophy of the stiff upper lip and a literal belief in Hell. We must realise that many countries think us barbarous because we beat children. Can we establish some points of reference? Possibly it may be acceptable to slap a young child. Though this may mean only that we, who were once slapped, have slapped in our turn and nothing very bad seems to have come of it. Perhaps we are disqualified from judging in this case. Perhaps also it is difficult to judge when permanent harm has been done to a relationship. At the other end of the scale, could it be agreed as unthinkable to beat a seventeen-year-old? Or any girl? Neither of these restrictions holds in every school, even today, but probably they do in most. Then where do we draw the line? And if our lady colleagues manage to maintain 'discipline' in mixed schools without canes, why cannot we also?

It is arguable that no child's posterior is sacrosanct nor even so important as to be given priority over the good of the com-

77

munity. Or that some boys are even the better for a beating (though the evidence for such a judgement seems hard to gather). However, if we grant for the sake of argument that some canings may do no harm—or even that they may do good —the presence of canes in a school will almost always mean that they will be used in some other cases than those postulated above. For that reason there are none in Wyndham. However, on the principle of not inviting trouble (among children already accustomed elsewhere to being beaten) that fact was not advertised in the earliest days.

What to put 'in place of striking'? A work party is much more satisfactory, though subject to the disadvantage that children may find it enjoyable to do some evidently useful work. Detention, as restraint of liberty, is a poor answer but it is unpopular, which may commend its use. No petty punishment is of much value. As the 'ultimate deterrent', a limited suspension from school has been used at Wyndham. It requires the authority, obtained by telephone and potentially very valuable, of the Director of Education and the Chairman of Governors, and is a rare occurrence. Perhaps surprisingly, it seems to be feared, even by those who might not have hesitated on occasion to absent themselves voluntarily from school. It seems to enlist public opinion against the offender, an effective sanction when communities are usually only too well informed about their neighbours' business.

This has been found useful. An extension of the idea has seemed appropriate in our Sixth Form College. If the school régime is permissive, it is most of all so at Sixth Form level. Most students respond well to this adult treatment. A few abuse it. Their offences of general slackness, lateness to school or class, failure to produce work, veiled insolence and resistance to authority are minor in themselves. None would justify suspension in a younger pupil but in him they could be more effectively dealt with. Our view is that, while attendance up to the Fourth, and soon the Fifth, is a legal requirement, not to be set aside except as a grave matter, in the Sixth Form it is voluntary, as between consenting adults, so to speak. After due warning, we are free to cease consenting. A recognition on both sides that this is so constitutes an effective sanction.

78

The large school has particular problems in relation to discipline. Apart from the fact that it brings together on one site the difficult children who might have been members of several smaller schools (and, if it practises streaming, concentrates them still further), there is potential trouble in the fact that outside the classroom any child or adult may be faced at any moment by people unknown to him. This is of course the situation of everyday life but not of the traditional school. It may be a cogent argument against the traditional approach to discipline. For if good behaviour is obtained only through restriction and fear of punishment, then the hope of 'getting away with it' through anonymity among the crowd must be strong. Perhaps we can only pin faith instead on constructive training.

How far does 'good discipline' include 'good social standards'? This question is dealt with in the next chapter. But we may first try to clear the ground. We have to disentangle present-day issues from the traditions of schools, still our unconscious models, which were set up several generations ago to do just this—to inculcate a common code of manners, as well as of beliefs, in boys and girls whose homes did not necessarily provide an impeccable training. Once more the regiment comes to mind. Only in military and in scholastic institutions has it been thought advisable to lay down with precision such matters as the length of a boy's hair ('not more than $\frac{1}{2}$ inch below a line drawn from eye to ear') or the width of his trousers ('not less than 16 inches at the ankle'). Both these last—genuine—quotations from a school's rules amount to saying: 'The fashions current among English gentlemen between the World Wars (not, be it noted, in 1900–14, when they were notably different) shall be observed in the Sixties in our school, if nowhere else; and the case does not require arguing.' Meanwhile, among girls it has been within a generation both obligatory to wear black stockings and an offence to do so; within two or three years, offensive to wear a mini-skirt and even more so to wear a maxi. It is hard to see all this as rational.

There can be no doubt that it is good (if it is possible) to equip our pupils with a sense of consideration for others, even

79

with the realisation that membership of a large community involves the individual in accepting some restrictions on his liberty, certainly with the sense that societies operate to some extent on the observance of minor conventions. But to over-stress the latter must be a mistake, if only because in the post-war world they have been changing so fast. If we, as teachers, identify ourselves with championing quite petty, indeed in some cases comically outdated, conventions, we threaten the position of the great principles for which, it is to be hoped, we also stand.

The particular problem of the comprehensive school, such as ours, lies in the widely mixed nature of its area. There are social standards which can and should be expected of many of our pupils—as their parents would expect them. There are other children whose parents know nothing of, or even despise, such standards. The problem is, in the short term, not soluble. Only one thing seems certain: it would be unwise, as well as impractical, to demand exactly the same thing at the same time and at any age from each member of the school.

NOTE

1 *The Observer*, 23rd November 1969.

Chapter Eleven

Social class and the common school

A cartoon in *The Times Educational Supplement* once showed a a young man, informally but conventionally dressed, and a boy, informally dressed indeed but in everything from his hair to his boots rather aggressively departing from bourgeois convention. To these two a front door has been opened by the lady of the house. 'It's Clive's teacher,' she calls back into the living room. 'He's come to talk over the problem of Clive's dress.' Behind her can be made out an exact counterpart, in every particular, of Clive, only some twenty years older.

To take the joke seriously, who should be criticised? Clive or his parents for having 'failed' the school? The master, that he failed to assess what can and what cannot be expected? Or the Local Education Authority for having failed to send Clive to a school which did not try to 'improve' him?

Perhaps it is beside the point to speak of anybody's 'failure'. If—and we must examine this further—Clive 'ought' to be dressed and to behave like his teacher, there is in the long term no need to despair. The campaign can be won. We may recall the ships which carried hordes of Irish immigrants in the middle of the last century to America. The miserable refugees from famine must accept their crowded, squalid conditions as the only hope of life. A majority, we read, died on the voyage. Among the wretches who survived was an ancestor of John F. Kennedy. His descendants must have had all the graces to learn. But all were learned in three generations.

Ought we to try to 'improve' Clive? But in what ways? That is debatable. It brings us face to face with the problem of social class. No English maintained school can altogether avoid it. In a secondary school it becomes, like race, much more pressing than it was amongst younger children. This accounts for the virulence of feeling in some quarters against the comprehensive (secondary) school, although the majority of all maintained schools (which are primary) are also comprehensive and non-controversial. Behind this feeling lie generations of snobbery but also generations of attempts to 'better oneself' which were not necessarily selfish or to be despised. Those who, under-standably, want their own child 'away from rough playmates', those who dislike on principle the idea of a classless society and those who fear that the pearls of education will be trampled underfoot by the undeserving (and so lost to others also) join forces in their opposition.

For the problem is academic as well as social. We have long recognised that our ablest children included some from poor and socially deprived homes, though we have held both that they were comparatively few and that we had adequate organisation for detecting them and for educating them along-side the more privileged. In effect, we said that education is intended for the middle class and, if you wish to partake, you must join it. The effect of this situation on the under-privileged child—how he was separated by his school from local friends and even, in a sense, from his family—was described by Richard Hoggart in *The Uses of Literacy*. Documented in much greater detail, it forms the subject matter of a fascinating study in *Education and the Working Class*.[1] The authors, who had trodden the same path as children, record from subsequent research how social pressures were felt by the able but under-privileged in the nineteen-forties. Selective places at eleven were gained to a quite disproportionate extent by middle-class children. Those of the working class who did win entry to Gram-mar Schools did so against the handicap of their family, their district or of a 'working-class primary school'. Once admitted, they were under continuous pressure, usually but not always overt, from the school authorities, to accept middle-class tradi-tions and standards of behaviour. Those children (apparently a small minority) who overcame their origin and made a success of their school career did so in nearly every case by positively conforming. When they were supported in this attitude by their parents, a happy as well as a successful out-come was possible. Where they were not, even success meant in a sense 'a broken home'. Among those who did badly in school, the clash of standards between school and home or district appeared to be the greatest single cause.

These conclusions must presumably give any Head of a selective school food for thought. Still more do they impinge upon us in a comprehensive. Given that we do not have (and do not wish to have) the sanction of exclusion for 'breaking school rules'—which, as we have previously argued, must almost by definition embody the trivial rather than the fundamental—and given that with us the under-privileged are not, as they were in a grammar school, a very small minority, is it even possible to make them 'conform'? And, if so, is it desirable?

To answer, we must consider values and priorities. We have to define what we mean by middle-class standards. Do we mean consideration for others? Is this distinctively middle class? It is true that there are many instances of self control, chiefly in such matters as bodily functions, the temper and the vocabulary, which some people observe out of respect for others, some simply because convention requires it. The effect is no doubt the same but, as in other matters, if we are to assess virtue, the motive is more important than the action *per se*. Would we go so far as to say that, if the action is based *solely* on convention, in other words, if it is an expression of etiquette, then it is morally neutral though it may be welcome as likely to ease social contacts?

Let us consider some other standards. Truthfulness, honesty, thrift, reliability, industry, chastity, sobriety, punctuality, tidiness—all these are highly desirable in a school pupil and, as virtues, they have been traditionally esteemed by the middle class. If the working class *as a whole* has not esteemed them, perhaps that makes a distinction. But perhaps the working class has not been corporately articulate so that it could not, as a class, set up any standards at all. The practice of these virtues is not of course confined to any single group. Since, however, all these are essentially *useful* qualities, they are liable to commend anyone to a superior or an employer. It has therefore been natural that many working men who practised them 'got on' and possibly joined a higher social class as a result.

Something more fundamental is respect for authority. All

83

kinds of school offences may be said to spring from a failure to recognise authority or to pay it proper deference. There can be no doubt that in a pupil obedience to authority, whether or not it is truly a middle-class standard, is extremely useful. Are we entitled to press for it unconditionally?

Why do we owe respect to another? Because he is older? Because he is therefore deemed to be wiser? Because he is 'in a position of authority'? In a secondary school, where some teachers are likely to be only a little older, some a great deal smaller, and some perhaps evidently less intelligent than some pupils, it may well be necessary to strengthen their position by a blanket cover of this sort.

> ... Take but degree away, untune that string,
> And hark what discord follows.

Even so, the spirit of our age is inclined to respect a man for what he can do or for how he conducts himself rather than for his appointment. This sense lies at the root of the modern movement towards a freer discipline. We should be happier if everybody in our school were respected, by right as a human being, than if a minority were accorded automatic deference because of their office. Soon, too, under American influence, we shall be revising our views about the need to use formal titles in addressing each other. When, in North America and in some English independent schools, the first name is used by a young teacher to his Head and by that Head in turn to his superior, this is a sign not of insolence but of mutual trust. The same could well apply—provided that it is by consent—to the relationship between teacher and pupil.

There is evidently no easy answer to our original question: should we expect our pupils to conform to middle-class standards? We hope that at the heart of our school lie certain values, Christian or humanist, and we do not particularly want, as schools once did, to turn out a type. But we must move to the academic aspect of class division and say a little specifically about our experience at Wyndham.

In an area containing social divisions more obvious than the average, we started with a problem. Our House system has had the particular aim of integrating districts and classes. But since a majority of the abler children come from better-off homes and *vice versa*, an academic organisation based on 'strict streaming' would give us a high degree of social segregation. That was an incidental consideration in rejecting it (or rather a consolation whenever the difficulties of mixed ability teaching seemed particularly pressing). At this point a tribute should be paid to the many middle-class parents whose children are our pupils. They have been faced with many unusual features in the school. Some have grumbled occasionally. A few have grumbled a great deal. Most criticisms probably reach the headmaster after they have passed through a sufficient number of mouths. If this is true, then amid all the brickbats it is astonishing how little adverse reaction there has been to the fact that 'because of mixed ability teaching my child is being taught in a group far less socially select than could have been arranged'. When the writer recalls how traumatic it was for him and his wife, less than twenty years ago, to send a five-year-old to a (carefully chosen) maintained school, his admiration is the greater.

But our groups are still not fully mixed (see Chapter 7, 'Streaming'). About one-fifth of any year-group is taught in 'slower forms'. This is a far cry from the days when one-fifth of the population at the top was selected and the rest 'found unfit for academic education'. We can say that these weakest children are taught in smaller groups than others, that they have form teachers specially selected for their skill and humanity, that the two (or three) slower forms in any one year are 'parallel' so that none can be regarded as the lowest. Moreover, the strong House organisation counters any social segregation. Nevertheless, we still have a 'weaker group'. Although social factors play no part whatever in its selection, not surprisingly it contains a high proportion of the socially underprivileged. Experience so far shows that only a minority of these children will gain 'promotion' to the main group of forms during their stay with us. And on the whole they will suffer disappointment and loss of interest as they grow up from eleven to fifteen—or sixteen, as it is for some and will soon be for all.

These forms are not easy to teach. They constitute a living argument against streaming. It is difficult for us who had our

85

own education in selective schools, who had no dealing until years later with the very slow, who have not known or have left far in the past the conditions of social deprivation, always to understand and care for such children. Sometimes their coarseness offends us. Sometimes we slip into the pettiness of thinking that if they show none of the institutional virtues, if their horizons and aspirations are pitifully limited, it is somehow their fault. Of course it is not. And how obvious it is that our task becomes harder if we cling to middle-class standards in the narrow sense. Clearly we must set before the children standards of humanity and compassion. We must hope that they learn something from our example. But we are only handicapped if we press for anything which can be identified as a social, rather than an ideal, distinction.

One further aspect of social class requires comment. This is the case of the child from a restricted background who has natural ability, enough in the old days to gain for him selection but little more. It is a sad fact of observation that he tends to lack intellectual stamina. He was in the past the Grammar School 'drop out'. When we realise that his home lacks books, varied conversation or other mental stimulus, this cannot be surprising. What we observe (rather helplessly) is a gradual loss of aspiration. He (or she) will probably remain in school for a fifth year, because this is done by the large majority, but it will be with steadily lowered sights. More and more he will associate, in and out of school, with the unconcerned. He will care less and less about homework (or about overcoming his particular difficulties in getting it done). Several such boys have become by sixteen almost defiantly anti-academic and anti-establishment, all the more so (we suspect) because they have a secret sense of having betrayed themselves.

Now here is yet another case in which outwardly visible middle-class standards are probably a hindrance. School stands for so many things which are alien to his home—dress, speech, accent, allegiance—as well as for the things of the mind in which he has at one time found appeal. How tempting it must be for him to 'damn the lot', to think that if teachers can care so much for the pettiness of wearing an outmoded costume or a tie, the other things they care about must also be worth very little. Many people may be afraid of surrendering things of importance by default. But there may be a greater danger in distinguishing too little between what is important and what is not.

NOTES

1   D. Marsden and B. Jackson, *Education and the Working Class* (Penguin 1966).

Chapter Twelve

Morals, ethics and authority

In schools, at least, the day of the preacher is past. The dogma he offered can no longer be agreed. Two principles still seem relevant to the education of the young: man's religious experience is an undeniable part of his history from which he should try to learn; and moral education remains of great importance, even though it is likely to be effective in inverse proportion to the amount of time spent in talking about it.

To deal first with the religious question. Education is patently incomplete if it says nothing about human aspirations after religious meaning and moral good. But opinion today is so fluid that there is no doctrine, supported by anything approaching an informed majority, which can be 'taught' (itself an inappropriate word) as either received wisdom or divine inspiration. It seems to follow that religious instruction, as advocated by the 1944 Act, is a mistaken survival. And while religious education is very important, both compulsion and the right of withdrawal are equally inept and harmful ideas.

For practical purposes of teaching in schools, we know that only a minority, usually a small one, of teachers can be found to teach 'R.I.' as conventionally interpreted. Their number would be further depleted if we could afford to subtract from it those of unenlightened, not to say illiberal, outlook. These facts, and the further one that very many teachers are observed by their pupils not to be regular church-goers, ensure that if 'R.I.' is taught conventionally it will be to the detriment of 'R.E.' in a broad sense.

The same applies to corporate worship, as prescribed by the 1944 Act. If this means compulsory participation in a daily service which is known not to be attended on Sundays, when it is voluntary, by many who organise it in school, harm is done to institutional religion. If the elements should consist of a pre-Christian reading, a sub-Christian hymn (such as 'There is a fountain filled with blood') and prayers composed, however beautifully, in the language of another age, this would seem self-evidently ill-advised and clearly harmful to the spread of a nobler view of Christianity.

Is there a solution? Perhaps before these words can be read by anyone else, a new Education Act will have provided it. The aim should surely be this. 'R.E.', as a religious and ethical interpretation of the world, should be taught through the conduct and expression of good men and women. As an important aspect of human knowledge and culture, it should be taught as a part of history. And school assembly, in appropriate sub-units that are not very large and do not span a great range of age, should present to pupils the wisdom of the past and of the present, both of those who, living finely, have found Christianity to be for them the greatest expression of truth, and of others who, also living finely, have glimpsed truth elsewhere. We do well in English schools to set aside a few minutes each day to worship. We do badly if we seek to give any close definition to that term.

At Wyndham we have tried to recognise the importance of R.E. by incorporating it into a subject known as Historical and Religious Education. Since our History was already taught on a basis of recurring themes ('Man and Society', 'Man and Technology', etc.), it was not difficult to introduce a new one—'Man and God'. And our daily assembly takes place in ten sub-units. Once a week, on Tuesdays, ever since 1964 we have received a simultaneous visit from seven clergymen—four Anglican, two Methodist and one Roman Catholic. In an area not so long ago riven by denominational strife this is very pleasing. If this chapter did nothing else, it should offer our grateful thanks to the busy men who have so faithfully and so long given up their time to help us.

All assemblies, as well as 'H.R.E.', are attended by all children. As they are conducted by many different teachers, as well as by pupils, they do not follow any fixed dogma. They are seen as an exploration of truth in which sincerity alone is valued. For practical reasons hymns are very rarely sung. In

assembly, as in other things, each House follows its own preferred style and pattern. Perhaps the most successful is the one
where members sit facing inwards in a hollow square. Notices
are first disposed of, then comes silence. Out of it the assembly
is conducted, most often by the Head of House from any place
in the square. After he has spoken, read or prayed, the hush
resumes and is sustained until the members spontaneously rise
to go about their business. We cannot say whether our
approach has aided the cause of Christianity, but we suspect
that a consistently conventional line would have done it harm.

In an earlier chapter we said that a school should be like a
family. As its children grow up, it will not wish to tell them what
to think. This may be questioned. But we can hardly do worse
than tell them what to think and then make clear by our
actions that we ourselves think otherwise. Children are very
quick to spot the credibility gap.

Clearly, the theme of permissiveness is raising its ugly head.
What is meant by this popular but imprecise term? Whatever
it is, it will normally be something derogatory. We conjugate
our verb as 'I am liberal: thou art permissive; he has no standards', but the line between the first two is uncertain. One
man may take a more indulgent view than the next over
homosexuality while the second is the more liberal about
hanging; yet each may be permissive in the eyes of the other.

And from what point do we start? It is no longer 'permissive'
to oppose burning of witches, hanging for theft, wearing of
cosmetics by women in public (though men must not do this),
nor to advocate the payment of unemployment benefit. But in
every case it was so. Is it (or was it) permissive to allow mini-
skirts in school? Or are they all right for a student aged twenty
or a teacher of twenty-five but not for a girl of twelve? It can
hardly be argued that it is she who provides the more dangerous
physical attraction. Is our judgement based on the fact that she
alone is 'under authority'?

Reaction against harsh authority accounts for so much that
we older generation dislike. Strikes are very regrettable. But
their deepest cause is a long period of absolute rule by management. Many actions of the Black Power movement are terrible.
But the movement has grown out of a long experience of rights

90

denied. Many recent deeds of students cannot be judged objectively without considering the background of an authoritarian education. Even as we deplore such an apparently senseless phenomenon as vandalism by modern youth, we must see it in perspective. Dr D. W. Winnicott has finely written:

> It no longer makes sense to deal with difficult adolescents by preparing them to fight for Queen and Country. Adolescence has to contain itself far more than it has ever had to do before, and itself is pretty violent material. When we think of the notorious atrocities of modern youth, we must weigh them against all the deaths that belong to the war they haven't had; against all the cruelty that belongs to the war that perhaps isn't going to be; against all the free sexuality that belongs to every war that has ever been . . .

Which would we rather have?

Schools, by their nature and their history, are upholders of authority. They cannot abdicate it when they deal with the very young. But they ought to question it often themselves. We teachers could hardly do better than ponder the reply given by St Anselm to the Abbot who complained bitterly about his novices.

> 'What, pray [said he], can we do with them? They are perverse and incorrigible; day and night we cease not to chastise them, yet they grow daily worse and worse.' Whereat Anselm marvelled and said, 'Ye cease not to beat them? And when they are grown to manhood, of what sort are they then?' 'They are dull and brutish,' said the other. Then said Anselm, 'With what good profit do ye expend your substance in nurturing human beings till they become brute beasts?' 'Nay,' said the other, 'but what else can we do? By all means we compel them to profit, yet our labour is unprofitable.' 'Ye *compel* them, my Lord Abbot? Tell me, I prithee, if thou shouldst plant a sapling in thy garden, and presently shut it in on all sides so that it could nowhere extend its branches; when thou hadst liberated it after many years, what manner of tree would

91

come forth? Would it not be wholly unprofitable, with gnarled and tangled branches? And whose fault would it be but thine own, who hadst closed it in beyond all reason? Thus without doubt do ye with your children. They have been planted in the garden of the Church by way of Oblation there to grow and bear fruit to God. But ye so hem them in on every side with terrors, threats and stripes that they can get no liberty whatsoever; wherefore, being thus indiscreetly afflicted, they put forth a tangle of evil thoughts like thorns, which they so foster and nourish, and thus bring to so thick a growth, that their obstinate minds become impenetrable to all possible threats for their correction.'[1]

All that was a very long time ago. However, schools have been slow to change. Here is how some behaved as recently as 1914.

'After the schoolmaster had ensured that his scholars were seated at equal distances from each other, he gave the command: "Position for writing". Immediately the scholars placed their books open with . . . the edges parallel to the edges of the desk or sloping slighty upwards from left to right. Then followed the command, "Prepare for writing". On this the children were expected to . . . sit quite erect and with the body parallel to, but not touching, the desk, the feet resting flat on the floor, or foot rest, but not close together. The left arm was to be placed diagonally on the desk, the elbow being about three inches from the edge of it and just clear of the side of the body. The pen was then taken up.'

The Abbot's policy seemed so right to him that he must have been astounded to have it questioned. Was it not so that the monastery had always acted? Let us hope that he came to see this fact as an argument for change.

NOTE

1 Quoted in Coulton, G. G. *Life in the Middle Ages* (C.U.P. 1968).

Chapter Thirteen

Democracy in school

Today we all want to be democratic (or if we do not, we are chary about saying so). If we work in a maintained school, we have been at least in name appointed by a democratically elected body, whether the LEA or our Governors. There, possibly, democracy may have to stop. For we cannot divest ourselves, as Heads, of our responsibility to run our schools nor invoke the wishes of our colleagues, our pupils or their parents as overriding it. This might seem to be sufficient justification for a great deal of autocracy in our actions. Few of us would find it natural to do like the headmaster of a large German *gymnasium* who recently retired as Head but returned after the short Easter holiday to full-time service in the school as an assistant. For we have been looked upon as autocrats and have tended, like our pupils, to fulfil expectations.

If we really 'went democratic' in schools, who should have a say in the government? Teaching staff, of course; pupils, within their degree, no doubt. Parents, perhaps. And ancillary staff? How should we balance the claims of a full-time care-taker and a part-time teacher? Should we take into account the dedication of the one (either one) and the relative unconcern of the other? And is 'having a say in the government' an appropriate phrase?

There are not many activities in a school which can properly be settled by a vote. Some questions are those of feasibility: it either is, or it is not, possible to make a given change in the time-table, and sometimes only the expert can give the answer. In most schools the headmaster himself will have to defer to this individual, though whether that is a sign of democratic grace or of laziness might be debated. Many questions are those of educational philosophy. The pupils might give a majority vote in favour of dropping mathematics from the time-table but it would seem unwise to act on this. Many affect only sections or departments of the school and therefore only certain individuals should properly be asked their opinion about them. Between these three considerations (and probably a good many more) much play might be made by a Head who wished to consult nobody about anything.

But consulting is different from polling. Decision by vote is seldom appropriate in school, if only because it is so very difficult to say precisely whose interests, being affected, should entitle him to a say. There is also a point when many teachers will feel that they have too much democracy. This point has often been reached at Wyndham. It occurs commonly about five o'clock when a staff meeting has already been in progress for an hour, the agenda is far from finished, some colleagues are in full flow and a majority of others are conscious of the clock, the children at home, the lawn to be mown, the marking and a great desire to see the question settled in any way so long as it be quickly. The irreverent thought that similar, though more august, considerations may sometimes affect a meeting of the Cabinet insists on intruding.

People do not always want democracy in this sense. But they do want information. If democracy implies giving value to the individual, few things perhaps make him feel so devalued as to find himself left in ignorance of matters which affect him. Now in a large (or perhaps in any) school it is quite impossible that everyone should always obtain the information he would like at the moment when he would like it. Nevertheless, the certainty of failure should not deter us from trying. A greater obstacle is the odium which we shall certainly incur by 'putting out too much paper'.

There does not seem to be any clear passage between that Scylla and this Charybdis. In a school like Wyndham, built in sub-units and without a large hall, there is a particular problem since no general assembly can take place. We add to that a greater difficulty, that our staff common room is so far away from where most people teach that it cannot be a daily meeting place in morning break nor even during our short lunch-hour. These are fairly testing conditions. Wyndham tries to overcome them by a daily Bulletin issued at 8.30 am to all the sub-units. A lot of information, as well as requests for action, can be found in this. From time to time separate Staff Bulletins are published. Bulletins also go regularly to parents and copies of these are available to staff as well as to the Governors. Every week a meeting is held of either Heads of House, Heads of Department or the full staff (the latter is not so frequent as a 'voluntary staff meeting' to discuss a particular question). For all these meetings the agenda is published in advance and the minutes afterwards. There is thus, as hinted earlier, a lot of paper available to read!

Wyndham gropes its way towards a truly democratic way of life and is still not sure how far it is appropriate to a school. By now there is an elected representative of the staff (additional to the headmaster and his two Deputies) coopted to the Governing Body. Thus the Head's termly report on the school is accessible to all staff. There is, as in many other schools, a Common Room Committee and this can call meetings of the whole staff (excluding Head and Deputies) at will. The experiment of putting the normal assembly of the whole staff under the chairmanship of a senior member so that the Head is excluded for a part of the meeting has also been tried—all this in the hope of avoiding the situation, endemic in a large staff, of too little open discussion and too much in private.

As these attempts proceed, and the Pupils' Council develops, perhaps we can suggest a compromise definition of democracy as it might be appropriate to a school at the present time. Not that everyone should vote, nor even be consulted, about everything. But that as much information as possible should be available to all connected with the school (not merely the teaching staff); that people should be consulted whenever their interests are affected; that while decisions are regularly taken by the Head or by his inner circle, whatever that may be, he should be prepared to give the reasons, so far as possible, on which the decision was based. It should be normal, as a democratic right, for staff or even pupils to ask for these reasons, even though it must be understood that out of discretion they cannot always be given.

It seems also wise, though it has its dangers, to recognise the right of appeal at any stage to a higher authority. Naturally, it will be disruptive if this is greatly used. But a good safeguard against decisions which either are or seem to be arbitrary is this right, openly acknowledged. It will apply, of course, to pupils—even though we must be very reluctant to question a colleague's authority. It will apply to junior teachers if they feel strongly enough to appeal against their senior. And it must apply to all members of the school *vis à vis* the Head. A practical application is to introduce the Chairman of Governors to a full staff meeting and make it clear to all that he represents and embodies a higher authority.

One feature of local government which has been reproduced is the 'public gallery' for meetings of the Heads of Houses and of Departments. Any teacher may attend, though he may not be allowed to take part. The opportunity has been used rather infrequently, which is not surprising since the minutes are always published. However, such attempts seem worth making in any large school at a time when participation is greatly, and rightly, in demand.

Chapter Fourteen

Towards flexibility: objectives

The large school, like the large firm, has probably come to stay. And for the same reason—we cannot afford anything less. Its Head is faced with a formidable variety of complications: in personalities, in plant and in activities, both within and without the classroom, there is a vast amount which he must try to understand. Having studied the material, he has to find his priorities. For his own rôle there will be a wide field of choice. As either administrator, scholar, teacher, thinker, technical expert, counsellor to his staff or public relations officer (if not even judge and executioner) he will no doubt seek the image which most appeals to him. Anyone observing him may note with interest which functions he delegates, and how far, and which he refuses to delegate. Both will reveal a good deal. For his school also he must choose a rôle. Shall it be the nurse of scholars, or of athletes, or of the weak, or of the community as a whole?

Obviously, these rôles do not have to be mutually exclusive. Many Heads will hope to see them all fulfilled. But, whatever particular bias a school may acquire, there would be a wide consensus today among Heads of big schools that they wish their own to be at once a humane and a flexible organisation.

This may be much encouraged by the attitude of the Local Education Authority. That in Cumberland has always stressed human considerations (so that, for example, the stranger who comes to be interviewed for a post finds a room already booked for him in a convenient hotel) and has given much freedom to schools. The block grant to meet annual expenditure, leaving the school to decide its own priorities, is a great asset. Even greater is the school's total liberty to choose its staff. Not only does this mean that selection is made by those who will actually work with the person appointed (for such freedom given to a Head will naturally be shared by him with the Head of Department concerned) but it makes for efficiency. Selection Committees cannot be assembled without notice. But on the Cumberland system an appointment can be offered and accepted within minutes over the telephone or even, to quote a recent example, late in the evening during a Whit holiday and on a railway station.

Within the school we showed in Chapter 4 how the need for humanity can be met. It is possible for each child to be well known to a teacher of experience, able to help him in any crisis. More difficult is to ensure full flexibility. Ideally, we want to provide every variety of course to any child who thinks he needs it. But if a single pupil asks to be taught Chinese, it is very unlikely that we shall be able to meet the request. Nevertheless, if we start from the premise, 'all hard lines in education are to be regretted', and make it our aim to draw as few of these as possible, we shall be moving towards our objective.

This was part of our purpose in virtually abolishing streaming. We have cancelled any barrier against entry to the Sixth Form, except that of willingness to work and the possibility of finding a suitable course (both these are, of course, comparative rather than absolute factors). At the Fourth Form stage, while the early comprehensive schools of the Fifties used to plan courses (academic, technical, non-academic, etc.), most have long discarded this rigidity in favour of free choice among subject options with, naturally, some guidance to ensure that the combination was rational. Wyndham, coming into existence only in 1964, had the advantage of other schools' experience so that these examples of flexibility could be incorporated from the start. We have, however, added something to them.

It is always a difficulty to offer options when practical and scientific subjects usually ask for double periods (where the norm is forty minutes) and most other subjects prefer single units. Because so large a section of the school (Fourth, Fifth, Sixth and Seventh years) is organised in options, this difficulty constantly crops up, It seemed sensible, as a move towards flexibility, to change the unit to one of sixty minutes. By this means, any subject can be offered as an option against any

98

other. Naturally, this creates some new problems. The school being a unity, we could not apply this system to only a part of it. All had to follow suit and we were bound to re-think the allocation of teaching time to every subject (not a bad thing to have to do). Moreover, since there were subjects, like foreign languages in the lower years, for which the longer period was unsuitable, we had to accept half-units in a number of cases. Consequently, a bell has to be rung every half-hour, even though many classes are to ignore it. But the overall effect has been that more variety can be offered to the pupils.

Again, when there is such a marked difference in physical strength between the child of eleven and the young person of eighteen, it seems absurd that they should be taught the same length of week. For several years this has been no longer true at Wyndham. All junior forms (the first three years) have one afternoon shortened as compared with seniors. In a rural area, where buses play a large rôle in the life of the school, this creates formidable problems of transport. However, they have been overcome.

First Year pupils are a special case. For them we originally shortened a second afternoon each week. However, in 1969 the opening of our Reception House brought about a more general change of routine.

This House had been part of the original plan for the school. For various reasons it was deferred and left to be built as a later instalment. There was no doubt in our minds that we should need the additional space as the school grew in size, indeed well before it actually became available. Nevertheless, the immediate success of our House system led us to doubt whether it would be good to interpose a stage for the child between his primary school and the senior House where he would, if he came from a small village, find his neighbours who had preceded him to Wyndham. Moreover, the Reception House was to take the whole year-group. It was twice as large as a senior House and this seemed all wrong. Finally, a period of only twelve months seemed too short to spend in it.

These objections should be stressed, partly because they were felt by all of us and partly because they help to ensure a cool look at the new House. We had disliked the idea so much that,

99

if we could have found another way in which to use the new building, we should have taken it. (Our liberal Authority, we could feel sure, would not have imposed its plan upon us.) However, two alternative plans came up against insoluble difficulties and had to be scrapped. Reluctantly we decided that we must accept the blue-print. It would therefore be only sensible to become enthusiastic about it.

In the event, enthusiasm soon became well justified. For the new House enabled us to tackle far more successfully one of the chief failures in flexibility, and one of the hardest of hard lines, in education. This is the transition from primary to secondary school. It is of course absurd that a child at the age of five should have passed overnight from complete inexperience of school to attending it for two sessions daily. But at least something can be done about this, in enlightened areas, by partial attendance before or even after the fifth birthday. Equally violent is the transition to secondary school, especially in an area where many of the primary schools are very small and where the only secondary is considered huge.

We had always recognised this problem and done our best to deal with it by visiting the newcomers in their primary schools, by having them visit us, by introducing them to their new House and its Head in the term before they were due to join us and, finally, by giving these new children an initial day consisting only of the afternoon so that they could absorb some new experiences and go home not too tired. But nothing altered the fact that the eleven year old passed from a small child's world, with few adults and perhaps only one teacher directly concerned with him, to one of great spaces, a maze of rooms used for different lessons, constant changes dictated by bells, the danger of getting lost and the fear of hundreds of new faces, some of them large and unsympathetic.

Most of this has been changed by the Reception House. We have sought to create in it a 'post-primary' atmosphere and introduce the child gradually to new experiences. He scarcely needs to meet older children before he wishes it. Friday afternoon is given over not to lessons but to sampling the varied activities which are possible in a well-equipped secondary school. Above all, he still comes under the care of a teacher specially chosen for interest in young children. And this teacher, with two or three others, will be responsible for a large part of the week's time-table.

We have experienced little more than a year of this régime but have felt convinced of its appropriateness. Even the fear that one year was too short has largely vanished. It is a very long time when you are aged eleven! During the year the pupils have had the chance to visit and dine in their prospective senior Houses. They seemed after twelve months ready to leave the nest. We are happy, despite our earlier forebodings, at the large step towards flexibility which the new plan has involved. The only fear concerns whether the special demands it makes on staffing will continue to be met, against all the counter-claims which exist in a secondary school under present-day conditions. This is further discussed in the next chapter.

Chapter Fifteen

Towards flexibility:
obstacles

This is a very exciting time at which to be teaching. Probably more is happening, and at a greater rate, than ever before. It is a genuine Renaissance. 'Bliss was it in that dawn to be alive ...' But new development means new difficulties, and those we face, through their number alone, are formidable. Here we are at the same moment seeking to abolish selection at eleven; to move away from streaming; to introduce to the secondary school a spirit of eager inquiry in place of docile acquisition of information; to re-discover the unity of knowledge by over-leaping traditional boundaries; to deal with the whole child, not the one who sees his teacher twice or three times a week for a subject labelled History; to deal with him humanely in the context of his home (no longer in antagonism with it); to create large schools because only in such will public finance grant us the variety and the costly aids to teaching which our pupils deserve; and yet to make the child feel that a large school is neither forbidding, incomprehensible nor impervious to the expression of his personal wishes. This last, of course, is a basic problem of western civilisation. Not only teachers but politicians, industrial leaders, priests and generals alike are wrestling with it.

So great can be the influence of an inspired teacher that in the microcosm of a small school almost all things are possible. The most pleasing example of junior education that comes to mind was observed in a one-teacher school of nine children in the depths of Wiltshire in 1947. No doubt the march of progress has since abolished it. The best class teaching was in Trondheim where an elderly woman had brought a large, mixed ability group of thirteen year olds to an almost incredible facility in English by the end of six years in which she had taught them single-handed every subject, including the basic Rs (Norwegian children start their schooling at the age of seven). But these are brilliant exceptions. For good or ill we have to deal in larger units and to coordinate the work of many teachers.

Education is rather like warfare. As a struggle against the forces of ignorance, or obscurantism, or the social sources of diseases (including, of course, affluence), the analogy is easy to sustain. But grant it in general terms and a particular resemblance emerges—that those in command are all too often trying to 'fight the last war over again'. This means no more than that our horizons are limited by our imagination; that the people of influence (including the parents who exert pressure on teachers) are conditioned by their personal experiences, mostly from an earlier day; and that, in a quite practical way, even those who do look far ahead can use, in order to achieve their vision, only the tools which are to hand. Just as the really radical writer or artist has first to create the taste by which he is to be appreciated, and it may be only in old age or after death that he wins fame, so the educationist cannot work out his dream until he has persuaded others that it is feasible. This is not true of the individual teacher, as we have seen. He (or more probably she) may work a miracle with a particular group of children, though she can be frustrated by an uncomprehending or opposing Head. But on any larger scale— of a nation, a Local Authority, a school or even a department within it—the recalcitrant materials to be moulded include, even more than buildings and equipment, the ideas, worn but not recognised as outworn, which already hold the field.

This chapter is written from the point of view of a headmaster and former Inspector of Schools. It is based on some understanding of the problems of a Director of Education and, proportionately less, of those of a Secretary of State. If we look from any of these angles at the question—how can we implement our ideal for secondary education?—we cannot avoid material problems. But let us for the moment concentrate on those of the mind alone. What are the main checks upon our thinking?

Success wins admiration, but this may last too long. And

103

successes won in a successful era have particular prestige. Here are some battle honours which may have become a handicap to us. They are: public schools, grammar schools, Oxford and Cambridge, the WEA and what Arnold Toynbee has described as the peculiar bent of Western civilisation, namely a 'penchant for machinery'. We shall examine them briefly in turn.

The first three have already been touched on and must not be further laboured (or belaboured). The public schools bequeathed us the idea that education was mainly about training for leadership (particularly through sport), character (in a Spartan sense) and social stratification. The grammar schools have adapted some of these ideas and the best, particularly some of the most famous direct grant, schools have stressed the pursuit of intellectual excellence. This fine ideal has been somewhat vitiated by the nineteenth-century view of *laissez faire* competition and the collective exploit—that so long as one person reaches the summit, we can all rejoice—but it is still fine. Oxford and Cambridge have of course been the admiration of the world. It is not entirely their fault that we are so enamoured of specialisation but it is still a pity. The WEA is one of the glories of English education (as the Folk High Schools are in Scandinavia). But even here there is consequent loss. Because in an age starved in general of educational opportunity certain rare spirits could find the sustenance they needed through a weekly evening meeting with a gifted tutor, we accepted for too long that part-time continued education would meet all the needs of the working man. (The Germans, despite the excellence of their *Berufschulen*, have made a similar mistake.) But the last of our 'successes' needs more detailed explanation, if only because its effects are harder to throw off.

Arnold Toynbee in *The Study of History* [1] comes to the conclusion that every civilisation has its peculiar bent or bias. Ours in the West, he says, lies in our penchant for machinery, for . . .

a concentration of interest, effort and ability upon applying the discoveries of science to material purposes through the ingenious construction of material and social clockwork—material engines such as motor-cars, wrist-watches and bombs, and social engines such as parliamentary constitutions, state systems of insurance and military mobilisation time-tables.

Nor is this new. 'Anna Comena, the Byzantine princess turned historian, sees our eleventh-century forbears in just this light, as appears in the mixture of horror and contempt which is her reaction to the mechanical ingenuity of the Crusaders' cross-bow.' One can imagine an educated but unsophisticated Japanese taking a similar view in 1945, or a Vietnamese today. It is by this means, of course, that we have won a temporary lead in the business of material civilisation. It may be that only by imitating our methods will the Oriental once more surpass us and regain his earlier superiority. But is this the stuff our dreams in education are made on?

What, indeed, is its relevance to our schools? It is this. A large school requires detailed organisation. This is mainly implemented by means of a time-table. To the making of this instrument goes annually a huge quantity of man (or woman) hours. The operation is probably bedevilled by the inclusion in the staff of part-time teachers who are available only so often and not on certain days. [2] But by far the greatest complications arise simply from the school's wish to offer to the pupils the maximum of choice. Gone are the days when a school would simply tell a child: 'If we have put you in 2A, you do Latin, in 2B German, in other Second Forms no language in addition to French.' Or, 'You members of 3C, as you move into 4C, will cease to take Chemistry.' They were easy days—for some people—but they are well left behind. By contrast, today we wish to keep the door of choice open. And of course, in a school of all abilities the task of providing suitably for each is infinitely harder than in one where all the less academic options could be disregarded.

The result is a long struggle for flexibility. In the first three Forms the problems are not so great as they will become later. There is only a small element of choice of subject by the pupil and only a small amount of 'setting' (that operation implies, of course, that the forms which are taught a subject in sets must be taken simultaneously and this freezes certain areas of the time-table). The kind of problem which we do face at this stage is this: 'X should take both the physics and the mathematics of P Form, Y should take both the french and the english of Q, Z should teach R rather than S because he is Head of the House in which the former are mostly placed, etc., etc.' The Reception House has added complications as we try to reduce the number of people who teach any single form in it. But it is at the Fourth Form that the real problems begin. By then almost all teaching is in 'Option pools', which means that a large number of groups must meet simultaneously (with resultant freezing of teachers) on several occasions during the week. This régime applies to the Fourth, Fifth, Sixth and Seventh years of the secondary course. So great are the complications in these years that no single teacher can perform in all four in the same year. Wyndham has had to experiment with teaching some Sixth Form groups after the normal hours.

Already we are in the grip of the machine. Every year something new, flexible and ingenious is invented and built into the time-table. But every flexibility of this sort creates a corresponding rigidity: the people required to carry it out become unavailable for anything else at that time. Thus year by year we become further 'computerised'. The phase is apt in more than one way. There is a growing feeling in the profession that these complications can be handled satisfactorily only by a computer. (It goes hand in hand with fear that it would take so much trouble on our part to teach the computer that Mrs Smith is not available on Wednesdays or that Mr Jones ought not to be risked with 4B as to destroy the point of using it.) The other applicable sense is this: once the time-table has been drawn up, it is almost unthinkable to make any major change in it for the year, simply because so much other change would be entailed. Only the most dedicated and humane, as well as the most efficient, teachers should be entrusted with the task of creating this monster. For they hold us effectively in their hands when they have done so. Their machine has taken charge.

A major factor in the situation is the specialisation of teachers in particular subjects. The better they are, the less sense it seems to make to ask them to teach anything else.

When they come to be replaced, it is a teacher of mathematics or of french, not just a good teacher, whom we have to look for. The Burnham Award offers its prizes to the specialist and practically ensures that we shall not be able to find all-rounders. This completes the straitjacket to cramp imaginative action.

It is a good idea to send pupils out on field expeditions, of a day or a week, in geography, history or biology, on visits to a factory, an agricultural show, a museum or a theatre, on projects in community service; to invite in lecturers, actors, ballet dancers or musicians; to set aside the normal lessons so that subjects may be taught as one; all these things are part of a modern education. But the operation is never simple—because of the time-table. We have always to assess: what will be the cost to other pupils, in terms of disruption to their work, if this group is allowed the desirable freedom of action? Fundamentally, it cannot be good for education to pronounce, for example, 'Every Monday at 11 am throughout the year you shall study Physics and nothing else', but this, in effect, is what we have to say. By the same token, it can only be to the detriment of imaginative teaching that it must always take place within the period prescribed by the school bell.

How to break out of this straitjacket? Here are some suggestions.

(i) To divide the teaching staff into senior and junior or grammar and modern. This, so far as concerns Wyndham (and probably many other schools) is not acceptable: we are one staff and we teach, if possible, throughout the school.

(ii) To accept that 11–18 is not a suitable organisation for a comprehensive school. At the moment of writing, unfortunately, it is true that the country cannot afford to staff a complete system of 11–18 schools. However, that is not a final argument: if the supply of teachers improves as it is hoped, the difficulty may disappear. (If we worked only on what was actually practicable at the time we should not even have raised the age of compulsory schooling to fifteen in 1947, to say nothing of future plans.) Let it be clear what the argument is: not that 11–18 cannot be satisfactorily organised according to current ideas; but that the flexibly rigid complications of the

107

upper forms seem to be incompatible with the informal flexibility which is desirable for the youngest children. There is a good case for saying that 9–13 plus 13–18 or 11–16 plus Sixth Form College is a more satisfactory organisation than the all-through comprehensive *under present conditions of specialised teaching*.

(iii) To adapt our teaching force (a long-term operation this!) towards much greater versatility. The argument about early specialisation in secondary schools is not merely about what is good for the particular pupil. It is also about the nature of the teachers whom we are producing for the next school generation. Our single—or double—honours degrees produce teachers prepared to teach only one or two subjects. That is unfortunate though understandable. But the students who emerge from Colleges of Education are almost as highly specialised. Indeed, it is often true that they offer only the same number of subjects as the graduate, but at a supposedly lower standard.

This is a most unsatisfactory situation. Yet the Colleges cannot be awarded more than a small share of the blame. The entire profession is orientated towards specialised teaching, partly for reasons of prestige but mainly because that is the way to gain a higher salary. Moreover, the normal entrant to a College of Education comes from school where, since the age of sixteen (if not earlier), he has been encouraged to specialise. It is late, even if he were willing, to re-convert him into a general practitioner. Yet many such people are needed in the schools.

Schools for the age-range 9–13 are being planned by many Authorities. In terms of the natural development of children that seems thoroughly sensible. But unless we are to accept that secondary education (and it is the content, not the method, which is at stake) will not begin until after the 'middle school' stage is passed, it is difficult to see how these schools will be satisfactorily staffed. If they merely reproduce, from the age of eleven or earlier, the excessive specialisation of our secondary schools, there has been little gain. What we need is the College-trained teacher willing and equipped to teach, say, four subjects to any child below the age of fourteen. The 'middle' and the 11–16 schools, and certainly those organised like Wyndham, would welcome him. He would restore the once-honoured position of the form teacher and give to young pupils a badly-needed sense of security and familiarity. Without him, the child-centred education which has been developed in the primary schools is liable to be lost in the secondary in a welter of specialised teaching. And with it is lost, or frustrated, much of the flexibility towards which we have striven so hard.

NOTES

1 Toynbee, A. *The Study of History* (abridged edition O.U.P.), p. 242.

2 At Wyndham in 1970 they totalled seventeen. This, it must be stressed, is a great asset (despite the resultant problems). It reflects the nature of the catchment area, which includes a higher proportion than usual of graduates and, not unnaturally, of graduate wives.

Chapter Sixteen

National needs in secondary education

We have by now a system of primary education which can stand comparison abroad. It is true that the size of our classes, at least in urban areas, makes us far inferior to the Scandinavians and reflects our unvaried bias in favour of the abler and the older. But in the century since we made elementary schooling compulsory (very late by the standards of civilised countries) and drove children too young into school in huge, virtually unteachable, masses, miracles have been achieved. Our infant schools have long been admired and, as for the junior, where the stultifying effect on teaching of the eleven plus examination has been removed, we can feel fairly satisfied. In the secondary field, however, we still lag behind our chief rivals in all respects except that of the standard reached by the few on whom we have concentrated our resources—less than half even of those originally selected at eleven. We may claim to have won the competition for which we chose to enter but even we ourselves now recognise (for the most part) that it was the wrong one. Too few of our children stay at school after the age of compulsion. Too little has been done to make staying longer seem to them worth while.[1]

Except where political dogma inhibits rational thinking, there is fairly general agreement that we must improve considerably the quality (which, in this context, means particularly the quantity) of our secondary education. More of our children should stay longer in schools, both for their own and for the nation's good. Dispassionately, we may agree that the way to achieve this cannot include setting them an examination at eleven which at least three-quarters of the candidates are required to fail.

Perhaps not much more can be generally agreed. But one of

the most notable advances of the Sixties was the promulgation of the 'Plowden principle' of positive discrimination in favour of the children whose need is greatest. Less widely accepted, but gaining ground, are these further ideas: that education should not be divisive of the nation; that boys and girls should normally be educated together; and that the good principle of continuity should not be carried too far, because children change rapidly into different people.

If all these ideas were accepted, we could still have considerable scope for variety in organising our secondary schools. The Middle school, the 11–16, Lower and Upper Divisions and the Sixth Form College (whether or not linked with further education) can all find a place in it. The only form ruled out on all counts would appear to be our previous standard model—the selective, single-sex, 11–18 school without any break.[2] Any combination of these forms, if adopted, would produce smaller units than the 11–18 comprehensive. We have tried to show that there is in the large school no insoluble problem of insensitiveness to either human or academic needs. But if we can avoid the disadvantages of size, so much the better. And we must recognise that the option-based education which we offer to teen-agers in England today conflicts with that appropriate to younger children—at least if we accept that the post-war revolution in primary school teaching should affect all pre-adolescent pupils. The larger the element of upper secondary education in a school (it is greater, obviously, in 11–18 than in 11–16), the stronger the argument for separating it from the lower secondary.

Despite Black Paper reactions, it seems possible to hope for a fair consensus in coming years over the principles mentioned above. The most likely remaining area of disagreement concerns how to cater for the exceptionally gifted. It has been argued (notably by Lord Snow in a recent article in *The Times Literary Supplement* [3]) that we should do best to follow what is said to be the Russian practice of setting up separate (almost necessarily residential) schools to educate the most gifted, possibly two per cent of our ablest children. This proposal arouses alarm among the staunchest defenders of the comprehensive school, on the grounds that to lose these pupils would

111

deprive the schools of pace-setters. The argument, however, deserves to be examined.

So small a loss, spread nationally, would not alone do serious harm. Indeed, whether or not the exceptionally able child would gain from segregated education, it may well be true that only in super selective schools of this sort could provision be made for rare subjects, such as Chinese is and classics probably must become. It has already been recognised that only in specially selected schools can unusual talents in music or dancing be suitably fostered.

Thus far, then, the proposal seems sound. But unfortunately it does not stand alone. We already have in England the dual system of maintained and independent schools. If all our children were to be educated under public arrangements, the loss of two per cent would not be serious. But it is not likely that that situation will arise in the foreseeable future. We have accepted for so long 'the right of parents to choose their children's education'—even though so very few actually enjoy it—that there would be little support for any move to abolish the independent sector. It will be eroded as the cost of schools, particularly of their staffing and their technical plant, rises steeply. But in the process it will be in a sense strengthened, as by pruning. The right to pay the ever-rising fees by covenant or by insurance policy will probably persist. Thus the taxpayer will continue to be involved in helping the well-to-do to contract out of the national system. The loss by this means of a certain number of able children is not very serious. But to lose the support of their parents is far more so: their number includes a majority of those who effectively, and many who actually, govern the country. So long as this loss continues, we shall have a maintained system less good than it ought to be— or than these men would tolerate for their own children.

So the proposal is not simple. We have to settle for a loss to the public sector of education of some seven per cent of pupils whose parents pay fees. Some of the latter represent, alas, a great deal more in influence than their number would suggest. We are still, in 1972, negotiating nationally for inclusion with other children of most of those in the selective bracket—fewer than half are as yet under the same roof as the less able.[4] The result of the last Election will not, to put it at its lowest, hasten the process. In this state of poverty of resources, attitudes inevitably harden. It is difficult to consider on its merits a proposal for removing a new element (however much of it might coincide with that of the fee payers) of children to super selective schools. Lord Snow's own son would have been a detachable unit under either scheme. But his father must see that only when we have reduced the loss from the national system to a mere two per cent (a distant prospect) can we feel that the rest—for whom he himself in the past has pleaded cogently—are not being downgraded. In the last twenty years we have made a beginning of prizing them. For many more in the future they will have to be defended.

Of course, organisation alone is not enough. It is just as easily possible to have bad comprehensive schools as bad ones of any other type. We need a philosophy to support such schools, a sense of the importance of all children to us as well as to their mothers and a sense of their potential, far greater than we have believed. We have argued earlier that we need freedom to re-think our curriculum. This implies a loosening of the structure of examinations set by universities in the interests of university departments. To make use of such freedom we need freely thinking and enthusiastic teachers. Many of these seem to be emerging from university departments and colleges of education. But this is still not enough. We need more versatile teachers particularly for the younger children and most of all for the new Middle Schools. And these will not easily be produced.

Our secondary schools have been geared to turn out specialists on the assumption that this is what the universities want. If the last years at school are spent on a narrow range of subjects, it is almost impossible to train all-rounders at a later stage. Neither the profession (in terms of status) nor our employers (in terms of cash) want the all-rounder. And so the vicious circle continues. Here, it would seem, is the chief professional, as opposed to administrative, problem of the coming years in secondary education.

NOTES

1 Those who wish evidence for these statements (which are scarcely
new or controversial) will find it lucidly set out in Chapter 2 of
Volume I of the Second Report of the Public Schools Commis-
sion (*The Donnison Report*).

2 It may well be that the organisation of Wyndham School itself
(effectively an 11–16 plus a Sixth Form College on the same site)
is too continuous; but the two component parts are virtually
isolated—and in a rural area some compromise may be inevitable.

3 *The Times Literary Supplement*, 9th July 1970. In a letter to *The
Times* on 12th July, the Chairman of the Governing Bodies' Association and the Headmasters' Conference made a similar plea.

4 Benn, C. and Simon, B. *Half way there* (McGraw-Hill 1970).
While not exactly encouraging, this book presents too rosy a
picture. Many of the schools listed in it as comprehensive are, to
the writer's personal knowledge, not truly so.

Chapter Seventeen

Conclusion: credo

> 'You taught me language; and my profit on't
> Is, I know how to curse.'

Apart from the enfranchisement of Caliban, what a lot education has to answer for. Looking back over only a hundred years of it, we can see why our forefathers were so unwilling to let the demon loose. For it has been responsible, among other things, for the following: the growth of the gutter Press, strikes, the ferment of unrest and malaise throughout the twentieth century, the fall of the western colonial empires, nuclear warfare. An equally long list of its benefits could also be drawn up. If we believe in education,[1] like the committed Christian we are apt to see its outworkings everywhere we look. The dying Mirabeau, according to Carlyle, gazed at the sun and remarked to his doctor: 'Si ce n'est pas là Dieu, c'est du moins son cousin germain.' We recognise the obvious benefits conferred by education and, if it has also been the cause of disasters, we can feel that these have been due to its misuse or, even more likely, to its partial and half-hearted application rather than to any fault inherent in the commodity.

Fifty years ago the Russian people were largely illiterate. By 1957 they were celebrating fantastic achievements in science which must have had a broad educational base. In 1914 almost all coloured peoples were backward and despised. By 1961 we had a Burmese as Secretary General of the United Nations. In the sight of history the chief development of this century might be not the passing of colonialism, not even the triumphs of science, but the spread of education which made both the others possible. Perhaps only education can prevent us from destroying ourselves through overcrowding. Yet it almost

115

seems in shorter supply than ever: we still look on a world where a majority cannot read or write. It is not certain that the spread of literacy is even gaining on the growth of population.

Untried indeed, we may say of education quite as truly as of Christianity. Yet it is essential to hope. One of the few good features in the General Election campaign of 1970 was the realisation of how many people were repelled by the over-weening, tendentious claims on their own behalf and the automatic denunciation of their opponents' measures which politicians still seem to think it their duty to produce. Suppose that the leader of any party had been brave enough to say: 'We have made a lot of mistakes and are prepared to name them (though in some cases we can tell you the extenuating circumstances). We shall certainly make more if you elect us as your government. But we intend to govern according to principles (which we specify) and to admit, so far as security allows, the mistakes we make even while still in power . . .' Probably he would have paid the price in defeat at the polls. But not certainly. If we study the huge advance made since Eatanswill, we may even hope to see the time when such an approach is dared and respected. Without the spread of education no such hope could exist.

Already we have seen the abolition of hanging, though it might be thought prejudiced to claim that as a battle honour for education alone (especially while it remains doubtful how far the measure has support outside Parliament). In the enormous, and world-wide, struggle to abolish colour prejudice it can scarcely be argued that the traditional religions have a proud record. Education seems to hold out a greater hope.

What sort of education? We look back over a century in which schooling has divided England more clearly than perhaps has occurred in any other country. The great hope of the comprehensive movement must be that it will unite the people. We need not pretend that there is not far to go. It is quite possible to have a divided population within a comprehensive school, as some research claims to have observed, though the phenomenon is surely less likely where the children at least enjoy the amenities of the same building and are taught by the same staff than it would be where they were permanently divided at the age of eleven. However, as Sir Alec Clegg pointed out in a noble speech on the 1870 Centenary, it is not enough to have included the weakest in one school with the rest. We must also care deeply about them.

Not all care is repaid. It has been our experience at Wyndham that while the influence of the school spreads gradually through a district formerly isolated, where people are still conscious of being different (whether better or worse) from the largely 'immigrant' teachers, some polarisation takes place at the same time. Some accept and are proud, if reticently, of the new facilities and approach. Others reject with ever more strongly embattled firmness. As teachers or headmaster leave or approach the premises in the evening or at a weekend, they are quite likely to be greeted by abuse from a group of young men, mainly unemployed, standing around our Youth Centre. Usually they include some former pupils. Caliban (as quoted above) described the situation. It is sad, but it is part of the price to be paid for generations of neglect. Society has denied these young men a chance (or they think it has, which makes little difference) and they are angered by their unemployment pay because they cannot be proud of taking it. For good or ill the teacher is identified with society and his motives are accordingly misread.

What are we to think of the spread of education when it means, as it inevitably does, the popularisation (in every sense) of culture? It is easy to dwell on the dark side. In spreading benefits widely, we have seen something lost. We may sympathise with a man of taste and kindly nature, Harold Nicolson, as he writes gloomily to his wife in war time: 'We shall have to walk and live a Woolworth life hereafter.' The danger is real. We cannot deny that the peaks of Athenian civilisation were rooted in slavery, those of the Renaissance in feudalism. But carry that view to its logical conclusion. Here it is, ugly and unacceptable, in the reply sent by Vita Sackville-West. From the lovely gardens she and her husband had created at Sissinghurst she writes: 'I hate democracy. I hate "la populace". I wish education had never been introduced. I don't like tyranny but I like an intelligent oligarchy. I wish "la populace" had never been encouraged to emerge from its rightful place. I should

117

like to see them as well fed and well housed as TT cows but no more articulate than that.'

Many of us who were educated before the war can recall how it was that we personally emerged from our 'rightful place'. It was due to education; and probably not to any generous public provision but to the work of benefactors, mostly private. Our less fortunate contemporaries of those days remained, as Lady Nicolson desired, inarticulate. We may wonder about the next boy or girl, the one who came after us and just failed to get the scholarship at the age of eleven or eighteen. Where are they today?

It is easy to smile at the counter-vision to that of Vita Sackville-West—of joyous, literate youth, forgetting all boorishness and striding purposefully towards the sunrise to the strains of a cinema organ. But unless we can hold on to some similar, if rather more sober, vision of the future, unless we can believe unshakably in our children, we in education are only, in Eliot's phrase, beating with our vans the air, now thoroughly small and dry. In a hundred years we have reached the point where public support for education, if by no means liberal nor even judicious (considering the value of the investment), is at least no longer mean. The need is for men and women of good will and of vision to make use of it for the future of all our children.

NOTE

1 For an interesting and amusing assertion that education, or at least intellectual culture, is in fact the contemporary religion of the West, see Morris, D. *The Naked Ape* (Corgi 1969), pp. 158–159.

Appendix 1

School and community: a personal view

i. *The Community School*

This subject is placed as an Appendix partly because I feel, like Browning in *One Word More*—'Let me speak this once in my true person'—and partly to set it in perspective. Too much can be made of the label Community School. When Wyndham opened, it was (according to a Survey published in 1969) the only purpose-built example in England of the genre. Certainly, no aspect of it interested so many visitors as this. 'What do you do as a Community School?' they constantly asked. And sometimes, 'How does it affect the teaching?'

The first question always seemed difficult to answer while the second is almost impossible. It was others, not we, who called Wyndham a community school and the name has no precise meaning. Probably the Cambridgeshire Village Colleges, begun in the Thirties, first deserved the label. They represented a radical innovation by uniting the child population (less a very small minority who went elsewhere to grammar schools) with the adults through educational and social use of the same building. Dual use was of course nothing new: the Evening Institute had for decades been housed in the elementary school. But it had never brought the community together any more than does the common use of a railway station or a bank. Henry Morris's conception of the Village College began to do this. It quickly inspired imitations, if on the whole rather pale ones. When adult education expanded greatly after the war, the Institute often became an institution in its own right, whether or not its Head was a part-time member of the day school's staff. (In the country he usually was; in the city, where Institutes were larger, he tended to be an independent Principal 'doomed for a certain term to walk the night').

From the dual use of facilities under separate management much dissension flowed. But it is obvious sense to make full use of scarce or costly plant. Failure to do so was glaring in Cambridge when I was a boy and one could observe the Colleges and their wonderful sporting facilities largely unused for half the year, though even at that time considerably subsidised by public funds. This illustrated the essential 'We and They' spirit which had dominated education through the centuries when it was the privilege of the very few, and the generations when it was only meanly doled out to the vast majority. To destroy this spirit, so alien to the second half of the twentieth century, was even more important than economically good. In that sense the concept of the Community School was only the logical outcome of a comprehensive approach.

We at Wyndham welcomed the idea of sharing our buildings with the public, though never doubting that this would give us a good deal of trouble. (The mere fact of being on view in our classrooms to passers by, or strollers through, inevitably made it harder to secure a good image for the school when nothing could be hidden.) But we saw this as only a facet, if an important one, of our main task, of making a school to serve the entire district. Even had our premises lain outside the town, like those of many schools, hardly accessible to the public, we should have wished to welcome all the children, of whatever gifts or social backgrounds. As part of our philosophy, we should have wished both to invite parents in to see the school and to discuss their children, and ourselves to visit them in their homes. This attitude alone might have created a community school. Indeed, since the catchment area of Wyndham, like Gaul, was divided into three parts—Egremont, Seascale and the villages—it was only in the first that the narrowest physical definition of community school could be fulfilled. Yet we felt ourselves no less identified with the other areas.

The Community School, then, is a house not made with hands. Its foundations are the abandonment of exclusiveness in the day; an acceptance by the public that this is our school, not simply the one that we are taxed for; and the liberalisation of the one-time night school into a Community and Arts Centre. Like the day school, the evening Centre has become comprehensive. In adjacent rooms are found soft toy making, the WEA literature class, the students of foreign languages or Astronomy and those who come simply to drink coffee at the bar with their friends. Side by side you may also see mother and daughter making dresses, father and son studying car maintenance. It is, as we said in our first chapter, like the mediaeval cathedral, a meeting place for the whole community.

Its philosophy is bound to be evinced, in one sense, in the classroom. It is reflected in attitudes and the relationship of staff with pupils. But it hardly affects the factual content of what we teach. Any self-respecting secondary school of the Sixties would study its environment, make visits to industry and invite in local speakers, whether clergy or business men, and very many schools would encourage their members to give service outside the building to the needy, the old and the sick. The content of our mathematics, our russian or our chemistry lessons did not particularly differ because of these attitudes or aspirations.

I would think that this view is essentially present today in a great many schools whether or not classified as community. It is certainly found in Bicester, where these words are being written. Whether there is gain in bringing all the facilities (further education, youth, swimming bath, library, etc.) under one management, as at Egremont, can be debated. The greatest advantage seemed to me to lie in the almost complete absence of friction between day and evening users when neither looked on the other as 'They'. The chief disadvantage consists of the erosion of the Principal's energy by too many calls upon it, since it is almost inevitable that he will see the school as his main task, not to be delegated, and the other cares as peripheral —to which he will give more time than he can truly spare but less than they deserve. Indeed, this attitude will be expected of him in the last resort by his employers, given that the school is compulsory for all while the other functions are voluntary and in truth affect only a minority. His emoluments will certainly reflect this view.

The problem is that if the additional activities are not conducted by the Principal, they may seem to lack status. If they are, they may be given too little of his time. Some Authorities

121

are now experimenting by placing the 'extras' under a Deputy Head. This certainly gives them standing but it is difficult to see how this man will satisfactorily divide his time between his spheres. A Deputy not much involved in the main work of the day time will not count for much in the Common Room. If he is deeply involved, the work of the evening must suffer for it (unless he has no private life). We have scarcely yet found the solution.

ii. *The Extended Day*

I finish with a glance at another aspect of dual use—the so-called extended day. Before Wyndham opened, there was considerable talk of round the clock use of the premises. This indeed did come about. But the concept of the extended day—if it were to mean extended for the same pupils and the same teachers—seems to me unlikely to develop on a large scale in a rural area. Already the period occupied by school plus journeys extends perhaps from 8 am to 5 pm (longer for those who live farther or stay later to take part in games, orchestra or plays). The need to eat must take children home (a second school meal in the day seems undesirable from the points of view of expense, enjoyment or family ties). After the meal, it is scarcely practicable nor, to me, desirable that any but a minority of pupils, and these the older ones, should return often from the village or the farm. In this, as in so many aspects of school life, it is good that a particular activity should exist. But a total view of 'the school and its members' must take into account that such an activity is neither possible nor even desirable for many. We should be mistaken if we expected to reproduce here the patterns which have won honour in the residential school or among adults in the Polytechnic.

As for the teachers, perhaps too many of them already in an active school will find themselves kept late on the premises by discussions (more often than for 'activities') and returning later in the evening to meet parents, to take classes or to rehearse some performance. For the lively and committed teacher the concept of nine to four is so inappropriate that it would be wrong to plan formally to alter it. Without any such plan, the premises at Wyndham were always a scene of some activity after school hours, and on Saturdays, frequently also on Sundays and normally for most days in any holiday. We returned there out of hours as to a natural habitat and this, though bearing hard on private lives, reinforced that spirit of enjoying the appointed task which helps to make a community.

This may introduce a final heresy. It concerns extra-curricular activities. We are all agreed that these are a valuable addition to a school's curriculum. But once more a dispassionate appraisal is needed. If we go back in history, it was the residential schools which fostered out of school activities. Of necessity. For, without derogating at all from the dedicated spirit of many teachers in boarding schools, we must recognise both that their pupils had to be occupied if they were not to rebel, and that some activities, mainly the aesthetic and practical, though at one time also the scientific and mechanical, would not have figured in school life (given up to studies which were reckoned more honourable) but for this extra effort on the part of their teachers. Grammar schools tended to follow suit. In the Fifties, when parity of esteem for other secondary schools was being acclaimed in policy and rather forlornly pursued in fact, extra-curricular activities, with uniform, caps and prefects, constituted signs of grace. In the comprehensive schools we adopted them eagerly as an expression of care for the children and the subject alike. At Wyndham in the opening year 1964–5, with everything to do from scratch and with an inadequate staffing ratio,[1] we all but killed ourselves to organise activities for almost all members. Gradually we came to realise that this scale could not be maintained and I at least to see that it was not even desirable.

It was interesting to be visited in our third or fourth year by Tim McMullen who, like me, had left the Inspectorate in the Fifties in order to lead a comprehensive school, and to hear of his similar experience at Thomas Bennett School, Crawley. And it is important to establish the reasoning behind this view. A school's first task lies in the classroom. Its second, if it shares the philosophy of Wyndham, lies in the community, most of all in regular contacts with parents. And if it is sensitive to the constantly changing needs of the times, it will be forever initiating discussions among its staff. These have to take place after school hours. This is one of the most marked develop-

123

ments in the present generation of teachers. Because we recognise the need for change, because we seek new ways of approaching the needs of children, and because both schools and departments are much larger than they used to be, a vast number of man-hours is spent every year in discussion among teachers. I think that it might be possible to recognise this feature of school life through a productivity agreement which lengthened the school year without increasing the number of teaching days in it, though I realise the difficulty of applying such an agreement to all types and sizes of school. But the purpose of this passage has been simply to turn a critical eye on one traditional facet of the extended day.

John Partridge in *Life in a Secondary Modern School* [2] has written perceptively of the loss to the prime functions of a school which is often entailed by such activities as the School Fair—if preparation and dismantling take place in teaching hours. This is one more illustration of the truth that in a school which tries to cater for all, the eye-catching occasion may not be the most valuable. The extra-curricular function wins applause usually denied to patient teaching or pastoral care. But it is not in things of this sort that our prime responsibility lies.

NOTES

1 This was due to some unfortunate circumstances and could not be alleged in any subsequent year against our generous Authority.

2 Partridge, J. *Life in a Secondary Modern School* (Penguin 1970).

Appendix 2

A note on teaching practice

Since teaching is a practical skill, it cannot be acquired without practical experience. This inevitably means in a real school since any artificial situation is unsatisfactory. It follows that, in their own interests, the schools must provide a training ground for students.

There are those who argue that training for the profession should be an entirely in-service operation. This is a tenable view, though the organisation of it looks dauntingly difficult. Almost certainly, we are not going to witness it in the foreseeable future. This chapter deals with the situation as it actually exists.

Every year, in a series of waves, an army of students descends on the schools. It is a campaign which would in any circumstances be very difficult to organise without detriment to the schools' normal work. As it is, the huge expansion in recent years of the Colleges of Education has hit the schools at a time when many of them are already suffering from the effects of reorganisation, new teaching methods and instability of staff. The uneven distribution of the colleges geographically makes it difficult to spread the assignments satisfactorily: [1] while many schools no doubt are not badly affected, some certainly receive a very large number of students and some classes are often in relatively strange hands.

This cannot be good for them. While there is stimulus in the presence of keen and resourceful students, not all are like this. But, even if all were very capable, the situation remains unsatisfactory. In most secondary schools the system of specialisation already places the education of young children in the hands of too many teachers. To add to them others for periods of a few weeks is very regrettable. But there is a

125

possible solution to the problem through a re-interpretation of the system of practice.

The policy evolved at Wyndham is based on these premises.

(i) It is wrong to remove a class for more than the occasional lesson from the care of its regular teacher.

(ii) Any teacher interpreting his task on modern principles should welcome the addition of a colleague who can teach or supervise a group, explain a difficulty to the slower member, repeat work for a child who has been absent, or take the bulk of the class while the regular teacher carries out any of these functions. Even when none of them happens to be needed (and that must be rare), there is value in many teaching situations in having a second adult present, most particularly in any teaching of English or a foreign language.

(iii) The main purpose of teaching practice is to exercise the skill of teaching. It should be helpful, not otherwise, to share the control of a class with a skilled teacher. The purpose is *not*, as it once was, to 'face the mob and find out whether you can control it'. That idea must certainly have been apt in the past, when classes in elementary schools (and we are all 'elementary', in the former sense of 'popular', now!) were huge and unruly. If students are allowed to think of 'riding the tiger' as the crucial test of their practice, this reflects both the horrors of those days and the idea that devising the content of a lesson is less important: that, too, was probably true when secondary teachers were expected to 'cover the ground' provided by a standard text-book.

We have circularised the Colleges which send us students and asked them to endorse these principles. Most have done so without hesitation. On such terms we are not disturbed by a large intake of students. It would be much more appropriate, and surely better for them, if they could have their practice in units of a whole term rather than for an artificial period of a few weeks. But at worst, on the conditions outlined they will do no harm to our regular work. If, as we usually find, they are keen, lively and anxious to give all they can to the job, we too will certainly benefit.

NOTE

1 One palliative is the system which operates between Wyndham school and Didsbury College of Education. To reduce the difficulty of the congested Manchester area, some studdnts do their practice 130 miles away at Egremont. Supervision is arranged by a senior member of the school staff. He works closely with the College, spending at least a week there in every autumn term, and acts for the relevant periods as if he were one of the tutors. Apart from a single liaison visit, which is much appreciated, from one of the College staff, Wyndham 'runs its own practice'. The situation is not very different from what has long obtained with post-graduate students who do their practice far from their university departments, but Wyndham is on a larger scale and operates regularly.

Index